Tanks and Combat Vehicles of the Warsaw Pact

Tanks and Combat Vehicles of the Warsaw Pact

Russell Phillips

Shilka Publishing
www.shilka.co.uk

Copyright © 2017 by Russell Phillips.

All rights reserved. No part of this publication may be reproduced, distributed or transmitted in any form or by any means, including photocopying, recording, or other electronic or mechanical methods, without the prior written permission of the publisher, except in the case of brief quotations embodied in critical reviews and certain other noncommercial uses permitted by copyright law. For permission requests, write to the publisher, addressed "Attention: Permissions Coordinator," at the address below.

Shilka Publishing
Burslem
Stoke-on-Trent
www.shilka.co.uk

Book Layout ©2017 BookDesignTemplates.com

Ordering Information:
Quantity sales. Special discounts are available on quantity purchases by corporations, associations, and others. For details, contact the "Special Sales Department" at the address above.

Tanks and Combat Vehicles of the Warsaw Pact/ Russell Phillips. —1st ed.
ISBN 978-0-9955133-2-7

Contents

Introduction..1
Tanks...5
Infantry Fighting Vehicles...39
Armoured Personnel Carriers..57
Anti-Tank Vehicles...89
Reconnaissance Vehicles..111
Self-Propelled Anti-Aircraft Weapons...121
Self-Propelled Guns, Howitzers, and Mortars..............................147
Multiple Rocket Launchers...171
Tactical Ballistic Missiles..189
Glossary...201
Image Credits...203
Digital Reinforcements: Free Ebook...207
About Russell Phillips..209

Introduction

The Warsaw Pact (more formally, the "Treaty of Friendship, Co-operation, and Mutual Assistance") was formed on 14th May 1955. Officially, it was created in response to the formation of NATO in 1949, and the re-armament and integration of West Germany into NATO. Another, unacknowledged motive was a Soviet desire to control Eastern European military forces. The Warsaw Pact was disbanded at a meeting of defence and foreign ministers on 25th February 1991. The Soviet Union was dissolved the following December.

The signatories of the Warsaw Pact were:
Albania
Bulgaria
Czechoslovakia
German Democratic Republic (DDR)
Hungary
Poland
Romania
Soviet Union

In 1962, Albania supported China over the Soviet Union in the Sino-Soviet split. They severed relations with the Soviet Union and ended active participation in the Warsaw Pact. In 1968, Albania protested the invasion of Czechoslovakia, and later that year they formally withdrew from the treaty.

The Soviet military had a deeply ingrained culture of secrecy, to the point that soldiers were not told the designations of the vehicles they used. Whereas most Western armies believed that crews should be familiar with their own specific vehicle, the Soviet army believed that once a soldier had been taught to drive a tank or fire a gun, he would be able to drive any tank or fire any gun. It was common for a subset of a unit's vehicles to be used for training, allowing the remaining vehicles to be kept in better condition. If a vehicle was especially secret, the soldiers would be trained on a different model, while the secret vehicle was kept in storage. In time of war, the soldiers would be given a short time for familiarisation.

Warsaw Pact weapon systems tended to be simpler and less expensive than their Western counterparts. This was partly due to the experience of the Second World War, when the German advance meant that Soviet factories were overrun or had to be moved. During that war, simple weapons that did not require complex industrial processes, and which could be produced in great quantities, were highly valued. Western planners generally assumed that a third world war in Europe would be over quickly, but Soviet planners wanted to be able to continue production even after extensive damage had been inflicted on the country. User comfort was a much lower priority for Soviet designers than their Western counterparts, but ease of use was of the utmost importance. Warsaw Pact armies consisted primarily of short-term conscripts, and many Soviet soldiers spoke and read little to no Russian. Thus, it was important that the weapon systems should be rugged, simple to use, and easy to maintain.

In a similar vein, Warsaw Pact tactics tended to be much simpler than those in the West. Although it is easy to dismiss such straightforward tactics, it should be borne in mind that they were based on the experience gained during the Second World

War, when a large Soviet army had defeated a smaller but technically superior German army. In the event of another war in Europe, the numerically superior Warsaw Pact armies would have faced smaller, technically superior NATO armies.

Soviet armoured vehicle designers used sloped armour to great effect for many years. Design of the T-34, which used sloped armour, started in 1937. Sloping armour increases the thickness of armour that a weapon has to penetrate. The effectiveness of sloping can be calculated using the formula Teff=T/Cos(x), where T is the thickness of the armour plate, x is the angle from vertical, and Teff is the effective thickness. The increase in effectiveness for various angles is given below:

10°: 1.02
20°: 1.06
30°: 1.15
40°: 1.31
50°: 1.56
60°: 2.00
70°: 2.92
80°: 5.76

In the above list and throughout this book, armour angles are given in degrees from the vertical: so 0° is vertical, and 90° is horizontal. To illustrate the dramatic effect that increasing the angle can have, consider the frontal hull armour of the T-62 tank. The armour was 102mm thick. The upper part was at an angle of 60° from vertical, the lower part 54° from vertical. A shell striking the upper part would have to pass through 204mm of armour, twice the thickness of the actual armour plate. The effective thickness of the lower part was 174mm — still significantly more than vertical armour, but much less than the upper, because of just 6° difference in angle. In the vehicle listings, where the armour is at an angle, the effective armour thickness is listed in square brackets.

Combat experience in Afghanistan highlighted some shortcomings in vehicle designs. The Soviet army was organised and equipped for a large-scale war in Western Europe or China. It was ill-equipped for fighting a counter-insurgency war in a mountainous region like Afghanistan. Vehicle crews often had difficulty engaging targets high above them due to the limited elevation of their weapons. This experience led to vehicle armament being given greater maximum elevation, to allow engagement of targets on high ground. This had the secondary effect of allowing some limited use against helicopters.

Tanks

The wartime T-34/85 was considered by many to be one of the best, if not the best, tank design of the Second World War. Despite development of new tanks with larger, more powerful guns, the T-34/85 was kept in service with the Soviet army until the 1960s, with some Soviet client states keeping it in service for many more years. The T-44 was accepted into service in late 1944 as an improvement on the T-34. This had some teething problems, and was only produced in limited numbers, but formed the basis for the later T-54.

In the late 1950s, Khrushchev, a proponent of missiles over guns, ordered designers to investigate the possibility of tanks armed with missiles instead of guns. Despite widespread opposition to the idea, work continued after Khrushchev's removal from power, and eventually led to the deployment of gun-launched anti-tank missiles such as the AT-8 Songster.

The Soviet Union exported many tanks during the Cold War, to Warsaw Pact nations as well as other countries. The T-54 and T-55 in particular were widely exported. Care should be taken when comparing the effectiveness of exported tanks against Western tanks. Export models, especially those exported to non-communist countries, were not always of an equivalent standard to domestic tanks, and the operating country would sometimes choose to use cheaper, locally-produced ammunition rather than buying ammunition from the Soviet Union. In addition, the armour on export models of the T-72 was less effective than that fitted to domestic models.

It is interesting to note that by the mid-1970s the Soviet army had three largely similar tanks in production: the T-64, T-72, and T-80. Despite the communist system of government, there were three major competing tank design bureaus, and each used political influence to get their own design into service with the Soviet army.

Western analysts predicted that the use of composite armour would change the shape of Soviet tank turrets from the curved shape previously used, to an angular shape similar to the British Challenger or US M1 Abrams. Turret shapes did become less curved with the introduction of composite armour on the T-64, but they remained far less angular than those of Western tanks fitted with composite armour.

T-34/85

The original T-34, armed with a 76mm gun, entered service in 1940. Many changes were introduced during the Second World War, the main one being the replacement of the 76mm gun with an 85mm weapon, the new vehicle designated the T-34/85. It was still an important tank at the end of the war, and production continued in the Soviet Union until 1950. Czechoslovakia began production in 1951, followed by Poland in 1953, with the Polish vehicles incorporating several improvements. In the 1960s, some T-34/85s were taken out of storage and fitted with the same wheels and engines as the T-54, as well as mountings for a deep-wading snorkel.

The hull of the T-34/85 was of all-welded construction. The driver sat at the front left, with a bow machine gunner to his

T-34/85

right. The fighting compartment was behind them, and the engine and transmission at the rear. The commander and gunner were on the left in the turret, with the loader on the right. All three were provided with periscopes; the loader had a hatch, and the commander had a cupola. On some models, the cupola could be traversed through 360°, and one model allowed the commander to line up the gun on a target.

External fuel tanks could be fitted to the sides and rear to provide additional range, and would be used before using the fuel in the internal tank. There was no NBC system or night-fighting equipment fitted.

The original main armament was the D5-T85 gun, but this was soon replaced by the ZIS-S53. Two 7.62mm DTM machine guns were fitted: one mounted co-axially with the main armament, and one on the right side of the front hull. These were fed from 63-round magazines. Some countries fitted a 12.7mm DShKM anti-aircraft machine gun on the turret roof.

Specifications: T-34/85

Crew: 5
Combat weight: 32 tonnes
Length: 6.19m (8.08m including gun)
Width: 3m
Height: 2.74m
Ground clearance: 0.38m
Maximum road speed: 55km/hour
Maximum road range: 300km
Gradient: 60%
Vertical obstacle: 0.73m
Trench: 2.5m

Armament:
1x 85mm ZIS-S53 gun
2x 7.62mm DTM MG

Armour:
Hull front: 46mm @ 60° [Effective: 92mm]
Hull side: 46mm @ 40° [Effective: 60mm]
Hull rear: 47mm @ 50° [Effective: 73mm]
Hull top: 20mm
Belly: 20mm
Turret front: 90mm
Turret mantlet: 250mm
Turret sides: 75mm
Turret rear: 60mm
Turret top: 20mm

T-44

Development of the T-44 was complete by 1944, but it was not produced in large numbers. Armed with the same 85mm gun

T-44

as the T-34/85 in a similar turret, it had a new hull, which was both easier to manufacture and provided better protection. The engine was improved, but the new transmission was unreliable. By the end of the war, it was becoming increasingly obvious that the 85mm gun was insufficient. It could not penetrate the King Tiger's armour, and could only penetrate the German Panther at under 500m. Possibly of greater concern, the Soviets had acquired an American M26 Pershing under Lend-Lease, and they soon discovered that the 85mm gun could not penetrate the M26's armour.

The Soviet army had a 100mm gun available, the D-10, which had been proven in the SU-100 tank destroyer. Experiments were carried out fitting D-10s in both T-34s and T-44s, the vehicles being designated T-34-100 and T-44-100, respectively. Both were found to be workable designs, but by this time progress on the T-54 had reached the prototype stage. Designed from the outset for the 100mm gun, this was clearly a better design, and so no further work was done on the T-34-100 or T-44-100.

SPECIFICATIONS: T-44

Crew: 4
Combat weight: 32 tonnes
Length: 6.07m (7.65m including gun)
Width: 3.25m
Height: 2.46m
Ground clearance: 0.51m
Maximum road speed: 53km/hour
Maximum road range: 350km
Armour: Up to 120mm

ARMAMENT:
1x 85mm ZIS-S53 gun (58 rounds)
2x 7.62mm DTM MG

IS-3

The IS-3 was developed as an improvement of the wartime IS-2, with a new turret and hull. Limited production began in the spring of 1945, but it was never used in combat. IS series heavy tanks were included in Soviet tank and mechanised divisions until the late 1950s, as well as being deployed in limited numbers by non-Soviet Warsaw Pact armies. Later, they were only assigned to special units, and were removed from Soviet combat units entirely by the late 1960s.

The driver's compartment was in the front, with the fighting compartment in the centre and the engine in the rear. The driver sat in the centre of his compartment, with a single-piece hatch cover with integrated periscope. The commander and gunner were in the left of the turret, with the loader to their right. The

IS-3

commander had a cupola, and a hatch was provided for the loader.

Long-range fuel tanks could be fitted on the rear hull sides. The IS-3 had no NBC protection or night-vision equipment. The main armament was a 122mm D-25 gun, which had a double-baffle muzzle brake. A 7.62mm DTM machine gun was mounted co-axially with the main armament, and a 12.7mm DShKM machine gun was fitted to the roof for anti-aircraft use.

Specifications: IS-3

Crew: 4
Combat weight: 45.8 tonnes
Length: 6.77m (9.75m including gun)
Width: 3.07m
Height: 2.44m
Ground clearance: 0.46m
Maximum road speed: 37km/hour
Maximum road range: 150km
Gradient: 60%
Vertical obstacle: 1m

Armament:
1x 122mm D-25 (28 rounds)
1x 7.62mm DTM MG (1,500 rounds)
1x 12.7mm DShKM MG (250 rounds)

Armour:
Turret front: 160mm
Turret side: 100mm
Mantlet: 200mm
Hull glacis: 120mm @ 55° [Effective: 209mm]
Hull sides: 60mm @ 60° [Effective: 120mm]
Hull top: 25-45mm
Hull rear: 60-90mm
Belly: 20-35mm

IS-10/T-10

After the end of the Second World War, development of the IS series of heavy tanks continued, eventually culminating in the IS-10, armed with a 122mm D-25TA gun. It was accepted for service in 1952, but the tank was renamed the T-10 after Stalin's death in 1953.

T-10M

The hull was made of rolled armour, divided into three compartments. The driver was in the front, the fighting compartment in the centre, and the engine in the rear. The turret was cast steel. The gunner and commander were positioned to the left of the gun, the loader to the right. Armament consisted of a 122mm D-25TA gun with a double-baffle muzzle brake, a 12.7mm DShKM co-axial machine gun, and another 12.7mm DShKM anti-aircraft machine gun at the loader's hatch.

In 1956, the T-10A added stabilisation for the main gun in the vertical plane. In 1957 the T-10B added stabilisation in both vertical and horizontal planes, and two infra-red searchlights, one to the right of the main armament and one forward of the commander's hatch. The T-10M was introduced later in 1957. This version had NBC protection and a new M-62-T2 gun with a multi-baffle muzzle brake. The 12.7mm DShKM machine guns were replaced with 14.5mm machine guns (KPVT in the co-axial mount, KPV at the loader's hatch). The T-10M was produced at two different plants, with incompatible parts, until 1962, when a single design was finally settled on. From 1963, T-10Ms were fitted with deep-wading snorkels, and from 1967 they were supplied with APDS and HEAT ammunition.

SPECIFICATIONS: IS-10/T-10 (T-10M IN PARENTHESES)

Crew: 4
Combat weight: 50 tonnes (52 tonnes)
Length: 7.04m (9.88m including gun) (10.6m including gun)
Width: 3.56m
Height: 2.25m (2.43m)
Ground clearance: 0.43m
Maximum road speed: 42km/hour
Maximum road range: 250km (420km with long-range fuel tanks)
Gradient: 62.5%
Vertical obstacle: 0.9m
Trench: 3m

ARMAMENT:
1x 122mm D-25TA gun (30 rounds) (1x 122mm M-62-T2, 30 rounds)
2x 12.7mm DShKM MG (1x 14.5mm KPV, 1x 14.5mm KPVT)

ARMOUR:
Hull front upper: 120mm @ 60° [Effective: 240mm]
Hull front lower: 100mm @ 55° [Effective: 174mm]

Hull side: 90mm @ 60° [Effective: 180mm]
Hull rear upper: 60mm @ 30° [Effective: 69mm]
Hull rear lower: 30mm @ 50° [Effective: 47mm]
Hull top: 35mm
Belly: 20mm
Turret front: 250mm
Turret mantlet: 250mm
Turret sides: 75-115mm
Turret rear: 60mm
Turret top: 30mm

PT-76

After the Second World War, the Soviet army decided that it needed a new light tank and armoured personnel carrier. Both were to be amphibious and share automotive components. This requirement led to the PT-76 light tank and BTR-50P APC. Prototypes were completed in 1950, and the PT-76 entered service the following year. The original PT-76 lacked NBC protection and infra-red night-vision equipment.

The PT-76 was fully amphibious, the only preparation for swimming being to switch on the electric bilge pumps (a manual pump was also fitted for emergency use) and erect the trim vane at the front of the hull. In the water, the vehicle was propelled by a pair of water jets, and steered by closing a hatch over one of the jets.

Main armament was an unstabilised 76.2mm D-56T gun, with a 7.62mm SGMT mounted co-axially. In 1962, the PT-76B was introduced, with the D-56T replaced by a 76.2mm D-56TM gun. The D-56TM was stabilised in both vertical and horizontal planes, had a bore evacuator, and a double-baffle muzzle brake in place of the slotted muzzle brake on the D-56T. The PT-76B also

PT-76B

had NBC protection for the crew, a modified hull shape to improve buoyancy in the water, and a pair of auxiliary fuel tanks, each with a capacity of 95 litres.

Starting in 1967, overhauled PT-76s had the co-axial SGMT machine gun replaced with a newer PKT machine gun. Improved communication systems and infra-red night-vision equipment were also fitted.

SPECIFICATIONS: PT-76B

Crew: 3
Combat weight: 14.6 tonnes
Length: 6.91m (7.63m including gun)
Width: 3.14m
Height: 2.26m
Ground clearance: 0.37m
Maximum road speed: 44km/hour
Maximum road range: 370km

Gradient: 70%
Vertical obstacle: 1.1m
Trench: 2.8m

ARMAMENT:
1x 76.2mm D-56TM gun (40 rounds)
1x 7.62mm SGMT MG (later 1x 7.62mm PKT) (1,000 rounds)

ARMOUR:
Hull front upper: 11mm @ 80° [Effective: 63mm]
Hull front lower: 14mm @ 45° [Effective: 20mm]
Hull side: 14mm
Hull rear upper: 7mm
Hull rear lower: 7mm @ 45° [Effective: 10mm]
Hull top: 7mm
Belly: 5mm
Turret front: 17mm @ 35° [Effective: 21mm]
Turret mantlet: 11mm @ 33° [Effective: 13mm]
Turret sides: 16mm @ 35° [Effective: 20mm]
Turret rear: 11mm @ 35° [Effective: 13mm]
Turret top: 8mm

T-54

Design work on the T-54 began in 1944. The first prototype was built in 1945, with low-rate production starting in 1947. Full production started in 1953. Initially, the T-54 did not have NBC protection, though this was added to later models and retrofitted to existing vehicles. Turret traverse and gun elevation was manual.

Main armament was an unstabilised 100mm D-10T gun, with a 7.62mm SGMT machine gun mounted co-axially with the main armament. A second 7.62mm SGMT machine gun was positioned in a fixed mount at the centre of the glacis plate, operated by the driver. A 12.7mm DShKM anti-aircraft machine gun was mounted at the loader's hatch.

In 1955, the T-54A replaced the unstabilised D-10T with the 100mm D-10TG, which had a fume extractor, stabilisation in the vertical plane, and powered elevation (but not traverse). This model also introduced a snorkel for deep wading and an automatic fire-suppression system. The T-54A was manufactured in Czechoslovakia and Poland as well as the Soviet Union.

The T-54B, introduced in 1957, added an infra-red searchlight and driving lights. This model was fitted with the 100mm D-10T2S gun, stabilised in both vertical and horizontal planes. All of these improvements were retrofitted to earlier models. The Poles designated this variant the T-54AM, and this designation was sometimes erroneously used in the West to identify Soviet vehicles of this type.

The TO-54 variant mounted a flamethrower in place of the co-axial machine gun, with a maximum range of around 160m. The T-54AK was a command variant of the T-54A, with extra communications equipment and a reduced ammunition load. The Poles made the T-54AD command version, which had an extension on the turret rear to accommodate the extra radios.

Some T-54As and T-54Bs were upgraded to the same specification as the T-55M, and were designated T-54M.

Specifications: T-54

Crew: 4
Combat weight: 36 tonnes
Length: 6.04m (9m including gun)
Width: 3.27m
Height: 2.4m
Ground clearance: 0.43m

T-54

Maximum road speed: 50km/hour
Maximum road range: 510km (720km with long-range fuel tanks)
Gradient: 60%
Vertical obstacle: 0.8m
Trench: 2.7m

ARMAMENT:
1x 100mm D-10T, D-10TG, or D-10T2S gun (34 rounds)
2x 7.62mm SGMT MG (3,000 rounds)
1x 12.7mm DShKM MG (500 rounds)

ARMOUR:
Hull front upper: 97mm @ 58° [Effective: 183mm]
Hull front lower: 99mm @ 55° [Effective: 173mm]
Hull side upper: 79mm
Hull side lower: 20mm
Hull rear: 46mm

Hull top: 33mm
Belly: 20mm
Turret front: 203mm
Turret sides: 150mm
Turret rear: 64mm
Turret top: 39mm

T-55

The T-55, introduced in 1958, was a development of the T-54 with a new turret mounting the 100mm D-10T2S gun, stabilised in both vertical and horizontal planes. The 12.7mm anti-aircraft machine gun was removed, 100mm ammunition stowage was increased, and an improved engine was fitted.

In 1961, the T-55A added radiation shielding and protection from nuclear fallout. The 7.62mm SGMT was replaced with the 7.62mm PKT, and the bow-mounted MG was removed. This was the first Soviet tank to be able to create smoke by injecting fuel into the exhaust, a common feature in later tanks. An NBC protection system and night-vision equipment for driver, commander, and gunner were fitted.

During the 1970s, a 12.7mm DShKM anti-aircraft machine gun was fitted to the loader's hatch on new and existing T-55s.

During the early 1980s, three new models of T-55 were introduced: the T-55M, T-55AD, and T-55MV. The T-55AD was fitted with the Drozd missile-defence system, the T-55MV had explosive reactive armour (ERA). The T-55AD and T-55M also had laminated appliqué armour added to the hull glacis plate.

T-55

All three new models had a range of other improvements:
- Thermal sleeve for the main gun barrel
- AT-10 Stabber gun-launched ATGM
- Improved fire-control system with ballistic computer and laser rangefinder
- Laminated appliqué armour on the turret
- Side skirts of steel-reinforced rubber
- Extra belly armour for improved protection against mines
- Improved NBC protection, adding protection from chemical and biological agents
- Napalm protection system
- Smoke grenade launchers
- Improved engine and suspension
- Improved radio (R-173)

A flamethrower variant, the TO-55, saw service with the Soviet army and naval infantry. The co-axial machine gun was replaced by a flamethrower with a maximum range of 200m. 460 litres of fuel were carried for the flamethrower, at the cost of reduced ammunition for the main armament.

Command variants of most T-55 models were produced, these having a "K" suffix (T-55K, T-55MK etc.). Command variants had extra communications equipment and an on-board generator. To make space for this extra equipment, fewer rounds for the main gun were carried.

Specifications: T-55

Crew: 4
Combat weight: 36 tonnes
Length: 6.2m (9m including gun)
Width: 3.27m
Height: 2.35m
Ground clearance: 0.43m
Maximum road speed: 50km/hour
Maximum road range: 460km (650km with long-range fuel tanks)
Gradient: 60%
Vertical obstacle: 0.8m
Trench: 2.7m

Armament:
1x 100mm D-10T2S gun (43 rounds)
1x 7.62mm SGMT MG (3,500 rounds) (T-55A: 1x 7.62mm PKT MG)
(from the 1970s) 1x 12.7mm DShKM MG (500 rounds)

ARMOUR:

Hull front upper: 97mm @ 58° [Effective: 183mm]
Hull front lower: 99mm @ 55° [Effective: 173mm]
Hull side upper: 79mm
Hull side lower: 20mm
Hull rear: 46mm
Hull top: 33mm
Belly: 20mm
Turret front: 203mm
Turret sides: 150mm
Turret rear: 64mm
Turret top: 39mm

T-62

The T-62 was developed from the T-55. Some components, such as the NBC protection and the fording and fire-detection/suppression systems, were carried over from the T-55. The engine and transmission were also the same, although engine cooling was improved. The T-62 did, however, have a wider turret and a longer, wider hull. The main armament was a 115mm 2A20 smoothbore gun, stabilised on two axes and fitted with a stadiametric rangefinder. After firing, the gun moved to an elevation of +3°30' and automatically ejected the spent case through an ejection port in the turret rear. Unlike later tanks, this was not a full autoloader, and the next round still had to be loaded manually. The T-62 was the first tank to mount a smoothbore gun, although the Soviet army had accepted a smoothbore towed anti-tank gun (the 100mm T-12) into service in 1961. The gun was relatively cheap to manufacture, and the APFSDS ammunition gave greater armour penetration, but was more expensive than traditional APDS. The 115mm APFSDS

T-62

offered penetration of 228mm at 1,000m. By contrast, the T-55's 100mm AP-T round could only penetrate 185mm at the same range.

Early production T-62s had protection against nuclear fallout, but not chemical or biological agents. Later T-62s added a chemical filter to provide protection against these threats. The T-62 was not used as a basis for specialised engineering and recovery vehicles; instead, the cheaper T-55 chassis continued to be used.

During its time in service, a number of improvements were introduced to the T-62. In 1972, the T-62 Model 1972 added a 12.7mm DShKM anti-aircraft machine gun over the loader's position. In 1975, the T-62 Model 1975 added a laser rangefinder over the 115mm gun. In 1983, Model 1975 vehicles were fitted with a new engine and the Drozd missile-defence system. Appliqué armour was added to the glacis plate, and the

R-173 communications system was fitted. These vehicles were designated T-62D.

Also in 1983, the T-62M was introduced. This had appliqué armour on the glacis plate and distinctive horseshoe-shaped armour added to the turret front. Belly armour was added to the hull floor to improve protection against mines, and rubber side skirts were fitted to provide some protection against HEAT warheads. In addition, the fire-control system was improved and a guidance system for the AT-10 Stabber laser beam-riding ATGM was fitted. This fired the same 100mm missile as the T-55, but had extra guiding rings to compensate for the wider barrel. Eight smoke grenade launchers were fitted to the right of the turret, and the R-173 communications system was added. The T-62MV added ERA to the T-62M in place of the appliqué armour on the glacis plate and horseshoe-shaped armour on the turret.

The TO-62 was a flamethrower variant of the T-62. The flamethrower was mounted co-axially with the 115mm main gun, replacing the co-axial machine gun. It had an effective range of around 200 metres.

The T-62K was a command variant, which first appeared in 1973. It had an improved navigation system and an electric charging system, and it carried four fewer rounds of 115mm ammunition. A command variant of the T-62M was also produced, designated the T-62MK.

SPECIFICATIONS: T-62

Crew: 4
Combat weight: 40 tonnes
Length: 6.63m (9.34m including gun)
Width: 3.3m
Height: 2.4m

Ground clearance: 0.43m
Maximum road speed: 50km/hour
Maximum road range: 450km
Gradient: 60%
Vertical obstacle: 0.8m
Trench: 2.85m

ARMAMENT:
1x 115mm 2A20 gun (40 rounds)
2x 7.62mm PKT MG (2,500 rounds)
T-62M: 1x 12.7mm DShKM MG (300 rounds)

ARMOUR:
Hull front upper: 102mm @ 60° [Effective: 204mm]
Hull front lower: 102mm @ 54° [Effective: 174mm]
Hull side upper: 79mm
Hull side lower: 15mm
Hull rear: 46mm
Hull top: 31mm
Belly: 20mm
Turret front: 242mm
Turret sides: 153mm
Turret rear: 97mm
Turret top: 40mm

T-64

The T-64 design introduced some radical changes from previous designs, which led to the engine, transmission, suspension, and automatic loader all being unreliable.

It was powered by a 5TDF multi-fuel engine using opposing pistons, making it relatively small. Main armament was a 115mm 2A21 smoothbore gun with an automatic loader and coincidence optical rangefinder. A 12.7mm NSVT machine gun was fitted to

T-64BV

the turret roof for anti-aircraft use, and could be fired remotely from within the turret. The turret and hull both had steel armour, with ceramic inserts for improved protection against HEAT warheads. Fold-out armoured panels (sometimes referred to as gills) were fitted to the sides to give added protection to the suspension. Two snorkels were carried for deep wading: one was fitted to the turret, the other to the engine. This initial version entered service in 1967, with production limited to about 600, all of which were later rebuilt to the T-64A or T-64B configuration and designated T-64R.

In 1969, the T-64A entered service. The Soviet army had acquired access to an M-60A1 provided by an Iranian defector, and this prompted the replacement of the 115mm gun with a 125mm 2A26M2 smoothbore gun, which had a thermal sleeve and was paired with an improved fire-control system. Smoke dischargers were fitted to the turret, and the turret armour was improved. A self-entrenching blade and fittings for mine-clearing equipment were added to the hull front.

The T-64B entered service in 1976. This had a new type of armour in the hull and turret, which was thinner than that used in previous models, while still giving equivalent levels of protection. Side skirts were fitted to improve protection to the suspension, and it had a napalm-resistant defence system. A new fire-control system was fitted, incorporating a ballistic computer and laser rangefinder. The AT-8 Songster ATGM was added, each tank carrying six missiles. This missile system could also be used against helicopters. Some tanks, designated T-64B1, did not have the AT-8 system. Some T-64Bs were fitted with ERA and designated T-64BV.

A command variant, the T-64AK, was accepted for service in 1973. This variant had an additional HF radio, navigation equipment, and auxiliary generator. It did not have a roof-mounted AA machine gun, and carried a 10m tall telescopic mast which could be deployed when stationary.

All T-64 models incorporated full NBC protection.

SPECIFICATIONS: T-64B

Crew: 3
Combat weight: 39.5 tonnes
Length: 7.4m (9.9m including gun)
Width: 3.38m (4.64m including side skirts)
Height: 2.2m
Ground clearance: 0.38m
Maximum road speed: 75km/hour
Maximum road range: 400km (550km with long-range fuel tanks)
Gradient: 60%
Vertical obstacle: 0.8m
Trench: 2.28m

Armament:

1x 125mm 2A26M2 gun (36 rounds, 6 missiles)

1x 7.62mm PKT MG (1,250 rounds)

1x 12.7mm NSVT MG (300 rounds)

Armour:

Hull front upper: 200mm @ 68° [Effective: 534mm]

Hull front lower: 100mm @ 60° [Effective: 200mm]

Hull side: 80mm

Hull rear upper: 45mm

Hull rear lower: 20mm @ 70° [Effective: 58mm]

Hull top: 15-30mm

Belly: 20mm

Turret front: 250mm

Turret mantlet: 250mm

Turret sides: 120-200mm

Turret rear: 60mm

Turret top: 30mm

T-72

The T-72 was initially accepted for service with the Soviet army in 1973, and was fully operational by 1975. It had a 125mm 2A26M smoothbore gun with an optical coincidence rangefinder and computer-assisted fire-control system. A 12.7mm NSV anti-aircraft machine gun was mounted on the commander's cupola. Unlike the NSVT fitted to the T-64, it could not be fired remotely from within the turret, and the commander had to open his hatch to operate the weapon. The turret had cast armour, up to 280mm thick, and the glacis plate had 200mm-thick laminated armour. Fold-out armoured panels were fitted to the sides to give added protection against HEAT warheads.

In 1979, the T-72A was introduced. This had a laser rangefinder to replace the earlier optical model, and a 125mm 2A46 smoothbore gun in place of the original 2A26M. Side skirts replaced the fold-out panels, and extra laminate armour was added, particularly to the turret. This model became known as the "Dolly Parton" because of the appearance of the thick extra armour on the turret front. Smoke dischargers were added to the turret, and improved night-vision equipment was fitted.

From 1985, some T-72As were fitted with ERA and designated T-72AV. An export version of the T-72A, designated T-72M, was offered from 1980. This variant was equipped with less-effective armour and a different NBC protection system. In 1982, the T-72M1 was offered for export. This had an additional 16mm armour plate on the glacis and improved turret armour.

The T-72B entered service in 1985, with a new type of composite armour. This was a variant of the armour used on the T-80U, and offered much better protection than earlier versions. This model was nicknamed the "Super Dolly Parton", and also added 20mm of appliqué armour to the glacis plate. It had a 125mm 2A46M gun, capable of firing the AT-11 Sniper laser beam-riding ATGM. Smoke dischargers were fitted on either side of the turret. A variant designated T-72B1 did not have the AT-11 capability. Both T-72B and T-72B1 were sometimes fitted with ERA.

In 1990, the T-72BM entered production, the last variant to enter production before the Soviet Union collapsed. This had the same fire-control system as the T-80U, Kontakt-5 ERA, and the Shtora-1 electronic countermeasures suite. Shtora-1 included optical jammers to defeat SACLOS missiles and a laser warning system to warn the occupants about laser designators and rangefinders. Kontakt-5 was an advanced form of reactive

T-72A

armour, capable of reducing the effectiveness of APFSDS rounds as well as HEAT and HESH warheads.

The T-72K was the commander's variant of the T-72. This had extra radios, and battalion and regimental command vehicles also carried a 10m aerial which could be erected when the vehicle was stationary. Similar variants of the T-72A and T-72B were designated T-72AK and T-72BK, respectively.

All T-72 models incorporated full NBC protection. They all had a self-entrenching blade mounted at the front, an unditching beam at the rear, and fittings for mine-clearing equipment. All models could carry a pair of 200-litre fuel drums at the rear (these could be jettisoned if necessary) and a deep-wading snorkel. Preparation for deep wading took 20 minutes. Once the water obstacle had been crossed, it took two minutes to make the tank ready for action.

Specifications: T-72B

Crew: 3
Combat weight: 46.5 tonnes
Length: 7m (9.5m including gun)
Width: 3.37m (3.59m including side skirts)
Height: 2.2m
Ground clearance: 0.49m
Maximum road speed: 60km/hour
Maximum road range: 480km (550km with long-range fuel tanks)
Gradient: 60%
Vertical obstacle: 0.85m
Trench: 2.8m

Armament:
1x 125mm 2A46M gun (45 rounds, 6 missiles)
1x 7.62mm PKT MG (2,000 rounds)
1x 12.7mm NSV MG (300 rounds)

Armour:
Hull front upper: 220mm @ 68° [Effective: 587mm]
Hull front lower: 100mm @ 55° [Effective: 174mm]
Hull side: 80mm
Hull rear upper: 45mm @ 50° [Effective: 70mm]
Hull rear lower: 20mm @ 55° [Effective: 35mm]
Hull top: 15-30mm
Belly: 20mm
Turret front: 280mm
Turret mantlet: 280mm
Turret sides: 120-300mm
Turret rear: 60mm
Turret top: 45mm

T-80

The T-80 was a similar design to the T-64 and T-72, mounting a 125mm 2A46 smoothbore gun with autoloader. However, it was powered by a gas turbine engine instead of the more traditional diesel. This was expensive and used a great deal of fuel, but provided excellent performance. Initial production of the T-80 started in 1976. Full-scale production began in 1978 with the T-80B. This had improved composite turret armour, and improvements to the fire-control system, including a laser rangefinder to replace the original optical unit. In 1981, the T-80B was deployed to Group of Soviet Forces Germany (GSFG). The T-80B was fitted with the AT-8 Songster radio-controlled ATGM and carried four missiles, which were fired from the main gun.

Two add-on armour upgrades were introduced. In the early 1980s, it was realised that 105mm APFSDS ammunition could penetrate the laminate armour on the glacis plate of the T-80B, and so 20mm of steel appliqué armour was added. In 1983, Kontakt-1 ERA started to be fitted to the T-80 fleet. T-80s with ERA were given a V suffix, and the existing T-80Bs were upgraded to the T-80BV configuration.

The T-80U was introduced in 1985, with a new type of laminate armour, Kontakt-5 ERA, 125mm 2A46M-1 gun, and a new fire-control system. It had the AT-11 Sniper laser beam riding ATGM system with six missiles, fired from the main gun. The gunner was provided with a thermal imaging sight, with a secondary monitor for the commander. The commander could aim and fire the NSVT AA MG from under cover. It also had an auxiliary power unit, which allowed important sub-systems to be powered without running the main engine. Production of this model was relatively limited. In 1988, a T-80U with a diesel

T-80U

engine, the T-80UD, went into production. This sacrificed speed for lower production, fuel, and maintenance costs.

From 1989, the Shtora-1 ECM suite was fitted to the T-80 fleet.

Command variants of the T-80B and T-80BV were designated T-80BK and T-80BVK, respectively. These carried extra communications equipment, but sacrificed the AT-8 Songster ATGM system. The T-80UK was the commander's version of the T-80U. As well as extra communications equipment, it had extra navigation systems, an auxiliary generator, and an improved fire-control system.

All T-80 models incorporated full NBC protection and fire-detection/suppression systems. They all had a self-entrenching blade mounted at the front, an unditching beam at the rear, internal and external communications equipment, and fittings for mine-clearing equipment.

Specifications: T-80B (T-80U in brackets)

Crew: 3
Combat weight: 42.5 tonnes (46 tonnes)
Length: 7.4m (9.9m including gun) (7m, 9.66m including gun)
Width: 3.4m (3.59m)
Height: 2.2m
Maximum road speed: 70km/hour
Maximum road range: 335km (440km with long-range fuel tanks)
Vertical obstacle: 1m
Trench: 2.85m

Armament:
1x 125mm 2A46 gun (36 rounds, 4 missiles) (1x 125mm 2A46M-1 gun with 45 rounds, 6 missiles)
1x 7.62mm PKT MG (1,250 rounds)
1x 12.7mm NSVT MG (500 rounds)

Armour:
Hull front upper: 200mm @ 68° [Effective: 534mm]
        220mm [Effective: 587mm] from the early 1980s
Hull front lower: 100mm @ 55° [Effective: 174mm]
Hull side: 80mm
Hull rear upper: 45mm @ 50° [Effective: 70mm]
Hull rear lower: 20mm @ 55° [Effective: 35mm]
Hull top: 15-30mm
Belly: 20mm
Turret front: 450mm
Turret mantlet: 250mm
Turret sides: 120-400mm
Turret rear: 60mm
Turret top: 60mm

TR-77-580 (Romania)

This was a locally built, modified T-55. Outwardly similar to the Soviet tank, it was longer, with six spoked road wheels on each side, and a distinct gap between the first and second wheels. A sheet steel skirt was fitted over the upper part of the running gear on each side.

The 100mm main armament was built in Romania, and was mounted in a locally designed and built cast turret. A 7.62mm machine gun was mounted co-axially with the main armament, and a 12.7mm anti-aircraft machine gun was fitted to the turret roof. Ammunition boxes for the 12.7mm machine gun were fitted on both sides of the turret. An unditching beam was carried at the rear of the hull, with a pair of long-range fuel tanks above it.

Specifications: TR-77-580

Crew: 4
Combat weight: 46 tonnes
Length: 9.25m (including gun)
Width: 3.3m
Height: 2.4m
Maximum road speed: 50km/hour
Maximum road range: 380km

Armament:
1x 100mm rifled gun (50 rounds)
1x 7.62mm MG (3,500 rounds)
1x 12.7mm MG (500 rounds)

Armour:
Hull front: 200mm
Turret front: 320mm

TR-85

TR-85 (ROMANIA)

The TR-85 looked similar to the Soviet T-55, but could be distinguished by the road wheels, since the TR-85 had six, to the T-55's five. It was based on the Soviet tank, with a new suspension and engine. The 100mm main armament was fitted with a fume extractor and thermal sleeve. A laser rangefinder was mounted above the gun mantlet. Boxes of ammunition for the 12.7mm machine gun were mounted on the turret sides and rear, with a stowage box on the turret left. A sheet steel skirt, ribbed for greater strength, protected the upper part of the running gear.

The driver sat at the front left, and was provided with infra-red night-vision equipment. The glacis was fitted with ribs and a splashboard. Two headlamps were fitted on the right side of the glacis. The gunner and commander both had infra-red night sights.

An unditching beam was fitted at the rear of the hull, and two extra fuel tanks could be mounted above it. The TR-85 was provided with NBC protection and a deep-wading snorkel, mounted on the hull rear when not in use.

Specifications: TR-85

Crew: 4
Combat weight: 43.3 tonnes
Length: 9.96m (including gun)
Width: 3.44m
Height: 3.1m
Maximum road speed: 60km/hour
Maximum road range: 310km
Vertical obstacle: 0.9m
Trench: 2.8m

Armament:
1x 100mm rifled gun (41 rounds)
1x 7.62mm MG (4,500 rounds)
1x 12.7mm MG (750 rounds)

Infantry Fighting Vehicles

The Warsaw Pact started to use infantry fighting vehicles in the late 1960s, when the original BMP-1 went into small-scale production. Most NATO armies only adopted the concept some years later, although West Germany was a notable exception, having deployed the Schützenpanzer 12-3 as early as 1958, followed by the Marder in 1971. In 1969 the introduction of the BMD-1 gave the Soviet airborne forces a similar vehicle specifically designed with their needs in mind, drastically improving their mobility and fire support.

BMP-1

The BMP-1 was first seen by the West on parade in 1967. This model was a pre-production vehicle, and there were several detail changes made before full-scale production began in 1970. Although not the first infantry fighting vehicle, the BMP-1 was certainly an innovative design. Main armament was a 73mm 2A28 smoothbore, low-pressure gun fitted with an autoloader. An AT-3 Sagger ATGM launcher was mounted on top of the gun barrel, and a 7.62mm PKT machine gun was mounted co-axially. Four reload missiles were carried for the AT-3 launcher: two in the turret and two in the hull. The BMP-1 had a vehicle crew of two (driver and gunner). When the infantry section was mounted, the section commander sat behind the driver and commanded the vehicle.

Eight infantrymen were carried in the rear of the vehicle, on outward-facing seats. Firing ports were provided, allowing them to fire while mounted. The infantry could exit via four roof hatches or two rear doors. One BMP-1 in each platoon normally carried an SA-7 Grail surface-to-air missile, which could be fired from the vehicle by opening a roof hatch and standing in the opening.

The BMP-1 was fully amphibious, and when in the water was propelled by its tracks. Preparation for entering the water consisted of erecting the trim vane at the front of the hull, switching on the electric bilge pumps, and replacing the driver's periscope with a taller one so that he could see over the trim vane.

The BMP-1 had full NBC protection, infra-red searchlights, and fittings for the KMT-10 mine-clearing plough. Vehicles in Afghanistan often had extra armour fitted under the driver's and commander's seats to give extra protection against mines, side skirts to protect the suspension, and appliqué armour added to the hull. These vehicles were designated BMP-1D. Some had a stowage box added to the rear hull roof, and a common further modification was the addition of an AGS-17 automatic grenade launcher on the turret roof.

Combat experience with the BMP-1 during the 1973 Yom Kippur War led to some improvements, and in 1979 the BMP-1P entered production. This replaced the AT-3 Sagger launcher with a new, detachable launcher capable of firing AT-4 Spigot and AT-5 Spandrel anti-tank missiles. Both the AT-4 and AT-5 used semi-automatic command to line-of-sight (SACLOS) guidance, which was more accurate and easier to use than the manual command to line-of-sight (MCLOS) guidance used by the AT-3. Unlike the AT-3, however, the new launcher could not be

BMP-1

operated from within the turret. Instead, the gunner had to stand in the open hatch to fire and guide the missile. The NBC protection and fire-fighting equipment was also improved, and six smoke grenade launchers were added to the rear of the turret. Existing BMP-1s were upgraded to the BMP-1P standard.

Command variants of the BMP-1 were the BMP-1K and BMP-1PK. These had extra radios and aerials, but the machine gun firing ports were non-functional. The BMP-1 KShM was a command vehicle used by commanders and staff at the regimental or divisional level. It had extra radios and a large telescopic aerial, but no armament.

SPECIFICATIONS: BMP-1

Crew: 2 + 9 passengers
Combat weight: 13,500kg
Length: 6.74m
Width: 2.94m
Height: 2.15m
Ground clearance: 0.39m
Maximum road speed: 65km/hour

Maximum road range: 600km
Gradient: 60%
Vertical obstacle: 0.8m
Trench: 2.2m

ARMAMENT:
1x 73mm 2A28 gun (40 rounds)
1x 7.62mm PKT MG (2,000 rounds)
1x AT-3 Sagger ATGM (1 + 4 missiles)

ARMOUR:
Hull front upper: 7mm @ 80° [Effective: 40mm]
Hull front lower: 19mm @ 57° [Effective: 35mm]
Hull side upper: 16mm @ 14° [Effective: 16mm]
Hull side lower: 18mm
Hull rear upper: 16mm @ 19° [Effective: 17mm]
Hull rear lower: 16mm @ 19° [Effective: 17mm]
Hull top: 6mm
Belly: 7mm
Turret front: 23mm @ 42° [Effective: 31mm]
Turret sides: 19mm @ 36° [Effective: 23mm]
Turret rear: 13mm @ 30° [Effective: 15mm]
Turret top: 6mm
Turret mantlet: 26-33mm

BMP-2

The BMP-2 was introduced in 1980, and was largely based on the BMP-1, with a similar (though more heavily armoured) chassis. The turret used aluminium armour and was larger than the BMP-1's turret. The commander was seated in the turret, to the right of the gunner. Like the BMP-1, it was fully amphibious and propelled in the water by its tracks. It had full NBC

BMP-2

protection and infra-red night-fighting equipment, and could create smoke by injecting fuel into the engine's exhaust.

The turret had a fully stabilised 30mm 2A42 automatic cannon, with a high elevation giving it some capability against helicopters as well as allowing engagement of targets on high ground. A 7.62mm PKT machine gun was mounted co-axially with the cannon. A launcher for AT-5 Spandrel ATGMs was mounted on the roof, and a ground mount was carried to allow missiles to be fired away from the vehicle. Export vehicles often had the smaller, less effective AT-4 Spigot in place of the AT-5. Three 81mm smoke grenade dischargers were mounted on each side of the turret.

The larger turret meant that the troop compartment had two roof hatches instead of four, and the capacity was reduced from eight infantrymen to seven (one seated behind the driver, where the commander sat in the BMP-1). Firing ports were provided, allowing the infantry squad to fire while mounted, and there were two rear doors. Roughly one vehicle in three carried a gripstock for a man-portable SAM system (SA-7 Grail, SA-14 Gremlin, SA-16 Gimlet, or SA-18 Grouse) and two missiles.

The BMP-2D was introduced in 1982. This model had deeper side skirts, appliqué armour on the hull and turret, and extra armour on the floor to provide greater protection from mines. It could be fitted with the KMT-10 mine-clearing plough. The extra weight of the armour meant that it was not amphibious. From 1986, improved stabilisation, fire-control, and internal communication systems were added to new production vehicles, and these improvements were gradually fitted to existing vehicles.

As with the BMP-1, there was a command variant of the BMP-2, designated the BMP-2K, fitted with additional radios and aerials.

Specifications: BMP-2

Crew: 3 + 7 passengers
Combat weight: 14,300kg
Length: 6.74m
Width: 3.15m
Height: 2.45m
Ground clearance: 0.42m
Maximum road speed: 65km/hour
Maximum road range: 600km
Gradient: 60%
Vertical obstacle: 0.7m
Trench: 2.5m

Armament:
1x 30mm 2A42 cannon (500 rounds)
1x 7.62mm PKT MG (2,000 rounds)
1x AT-5 Spandrel ATGM (1 + 4 missiles)

Armour:
Hull: 5-19mm
Turret: 23mm-33mm

BMP-3

The BMP-3 entered service in 1990. It used aluminium armour, with spaced steel-aluminium armour on the front and hull floor. Like earlier models, it was amphibious, had full NBC protection, and could create smoke by injecting fuel into the exhaust. Unlike earlier models, it was propelled in the water by two water jets. A self-entrenching blade was fitted under the bow.

BMP-3

A 2A70 100mm rifled gun, 2A72 30mm cannon, and 7.62mm PKT machine gun were mounted in the turret, with a 7.62mm PKT forward-firing machine gun on each side of the hull. The three turret weapons were all mounted in a single assembly, designated 2K23, which was stabilised in the horizontal and vertical planes. A laser rangefinder was fitted, which fed data to a computerised fire-control system. Elevation was -5 to +60°, allowing the 30mm cannon to engage helicopters as well as targets on high ground. The 100mm gun fired HE-FRAG (loaded from an autoloader) and the AT-10 Stabber ATGM (loaded manually).

The BMP-3 had a vehicle crew of three (driver, gunner, commander) and normally carried seven infantrymen (two in the front, five in the rear). If required, an extra two infantrymen could be accommodated in the rear. There were two large rear doors for entry and exit, and two roof hatches above the troop compartment.

Specifications: BMP-3

Crew: 3 + 7 passengers
Combat weight: 18,700kg
Length: 6.72m
Width: 3.15m
Height: 3.57m
Ground clearance: 0.19 - 0.51m (adjustable)
Maximum road speed: 70km/hour
Maximum road range: 800km
Gradient: 60%
Vertical obstacle: 0.8m
Trench: 2.5m
Armour (max): 35mm (estimated)

Armament:
1x 2A70 100mm gun (40 rounds, 8 missiles)
2A72 30mm cannon (500 rounds)
3x 7.62mm PKT MG (6,000 rounds)

BMD-1

The BMD-1 entered service in 1969, and was first seen in public in 1973. It was air-portable by aeroplane (An-12, An-22, Il-76, An-124) or helicopter (Mi-6 and Mi-26), and could also be dropped by parachute. Initially the vehicle and crew were parachuted separately. After tests conducted during the 1970s, this was changed and the vehicle was dropped with the driver and gunner seated inside.

BMD-1

The hull was made of welded aluminium, with the driver in the front centre and the commander in the front left. To the right of the driver was a machine gun operator, who operated the two bow-mounted 7.62mm PKT machine guns. The turret was the same design as that used on the BMP-1. The rear hull, housing the airborne squad, had a single roof hatch with a concertina-type cover. Unlike the BMP-1, the BMD-1 did not have rear doors, so the roof hatch was the only means of entry to, and exit from, the rear compartment.

The BMD-1 was fully amphibious, and was propelled in the water by a pair of water jets at the rear of the hull. A trim vane was erected at the front of the hull before entering the water. It was fitted with a PAZ NBC system, infra-red driving lights and a white-light searchlight, which could be replaced with an infra-red searchlight. Main armament was a 2A28 73mm smoothbore, low-pressure gun fitted with an autoloader. An AT-3 Sagger ATGM launcher was mounted on top of the gun barrel, and a

7.62mm PKT machine gun was mounted co-axially. Two reload missiles were stowed in the turret.

The BMD-1K was the command variant, with extra communications facilities. The BMD-1M was first seen in 1980. This model had improved ventilation, and could be identified by a vent grill on the bow. Another variant, the BMD-1P, had a pintle-mounted launcher for the AT-4 Spigot ATGM instead of the AT-3 launcher. The AT-4 launcher could be fitted with a night sight.

Some vehicles in Afghanistan were fitted with an 82mm mortar in the rear troop compartment, firing rearwards.

SPECIFICATIONS: BMD-1

Crew: 2 + 5 passengers
Combat weight: 7,500kg
Length: 5.4m
Width: 2.63m
Height: 1.62 - 1.97m
Ground clearance: 0.1 - 0.45m
Maximum road speed: 70km/hour
Maximum road range: 320km
Gradient: 60%
Vertical obstacle: 0.8m
Trench: 1.6m

ARMAMENT:
1x 2A28 73mm gun (40 rounds)
3x 7.62mm PKT MG (6,000 rounds)
1x AT-3 Sagger ATGM (1 + 3 missiles)

ARMOUR (MAX):
Hull: 15mm
Turret: 23mm

BMD-2

The first prototype of the BMD-2 was completed in 1985, with production starting in 1989. It was initially believed that they were rebuilt BMD-1s, but in fact the vehicles were new. The hull was similar to that of the BMD-1, though one of the bow-mounted PKT machine guns was removed, leaving only the one on the right side of the hull.

BMD-2

The turret, however, was radically different to that on the BMD-1. Main armament was a 2A42 30mm automatic cannon, stabilised in both vertical and horizontal planes, and capable of engaging helicopters as well as ground targets. An infra-red and white-light searchlight was fitted, and a 7.62mm PKT machine gun was mounted co-axially with the cannon. A pintle mount was fitted to the roof of the turret, on which an AT-4 Spigot or AT-5 Spandrel ATGM launcher was mounted. A ground mount was carried to allow missiles to be launched away from the vehicle itself.

Like the BMD-1, the BMD-2 was air-portable, air-droppable, fully amphibious, and had full NBC protection.

Specifications: BMD-2

Crew: 3 + 4 passengers
Combat weight: 8,225kg
Length: 5.91m
Width: 2.63m
Height: 1.97m
Ground clearance: 0.1 - 0.45m
Maximum road speed: 60km/hour
Maximum road range: 500km
Gradient: 60%
Vertical obstacle: 0.6m
Trench: 1.2m

Armament:
1x 2A42 30mm cannon (300 rounds)
2x 7.62mm PKT MG (3,000 rounds)
1x AT-4 Spigot or AT-5 Spandrel ATGM (1 + 3 missiles)

Armour (max):
Hull: 15mm
Turret: 23mm

BMD-3

The BMD-3 entered service with Soviet airborne units in 1990, then later with naval infantry units. It had a new hull married to the turret of the BMP-2. The hull had aluminium armour, while the turret's armour was steel. The seats for the driver and two front gunners hung from the roof, rather than being mounted on the floor. This arrangement improved crew survivability in the event that the vehicle hit an anti-tank mine.

The hull mounted an AG-17 30mm automatic grenade launcher in the left front, and a 5.45mm RPKS machine gun in the right front. These weapons were operated by two of the mounted infantry, seated to either side of the driver. Both weapons could be quickly removed for use by the dismounted infantry squad.

The two-man turret had a 2A42 30mm automatic cannon, stabilised in both vertical and horizontal planes. It had high elevation and was capable of engaging helicopters as well as ground targets. An infra-red searchlight was fitted, and a 7.62mm PKT machine gun was mounted co-axially with the cannon. An AT-4 Spigot or AT-5 Spandrel ATGM launcher was mounted on the turret roof. Each side of the turret had three 81mm smoke grenade dischargers, and the vehicle could also produce smoke by injecting fuel into the exhaust manifold.

The BMD-3 vehicle crew consisted of driver, gunner, and commander, although the commander normally dismounted with the infantry. Four infantry were carried: two in the front, who operated the AG-17 and RPKS, and two in the rear, who were provided with firing ports in the hull. An extra three infantry could be carried for short distances; these were placed immediately to the rear of the turret, with the roof hatch open.

Like earlier BMD models, the BMD-3 was air-portable, air-droppable, and had full NBC protection. The amphibious capabilities of the BMD-3 were significantly greater than the earlier models—hence the adoption of the vehicle by the naval infantry.

Specifications: BMD-3

Crew: 3 + 4 passengers
Combat weight: 13,200kg
Length: 6.36m
Width: 3.13m
Height: 2.17m
Ground clearance: 0.45m
Maximum road speed: 70km/hour
Maximum road range: 500km
Gradient: 60%
Vertical obstacle: 0.6m
Armour: Proof against small arms and shell splinters

Armament:
1x 2A42 30mm cannon (860 rounds)
1x 7.62mm PKT MG (2,000 rounds)
1x AT-4 Spigot or AT-5 Spandrel ATGM (1 + 4 missiles)
1x AG-17 30mm automatic grenade launcher (550 rounds)
1x 5.45mm RPKS MG (2,160 rounds)

BMP-23 (Bulgaria)

When this was first spotted by the West, it was thought to be based on the 2S1 self-propelled howitzer. In fact, it was based on the MT-LB, which shares many automotive parts with the 2S1.

The welded hull and turret had sufficient armour to provide protection against small arms fire and shell splinters. The driver sat at the front on the left, with one of the infantry squad to his right. He was provided with a hatch cover and three periscopes, one of which could be replaced with a passive night-vision device.

The engine compartment was immediately behind these two men, with roof hatches for access. Behind the engine, a two-man power-operated turret was fitted. The gunner sat in the left of the turret, and the commander in the right. The main armament was an unstabilised 23mm cannon of the same type as used on the ZU-23-2 AA gun. A 7.62mm PKT machine gun was mounted co-axially. A launcher for an AT-3 Sagger ATGM was mounted on the turret roof. This could be fired from within the turret, and a further three missiles were carried as reloads. The gunner had passive night sights, and the commander had a night searchlight, controlled from within the turret.

The BMP-23 could carry six men in the rear infantry compartment, accessed via a pair of rear doors or two roof hatches. Eight firing ports were provided in the rear compartment, three on each side, and one in each door.

The BMP-23 was fully amphibious, propelled in the water by its tracks. Before entering the water, bilge pumps were switched on, the trim vane erected, and the driver's periscope replaced by an extendable one that enabled him to see over the trim vane. It had NBC protection and could lay a smokescreen by injecting diesel into the exhaust.

SPECIFICATIONS: BMP-23

Crew: 3 + 7 passengers
Combat weight: 15,200kg
Length: 7.29m
Width: 2.85m
Height: 2.53m
Ground clearance: 0.4m
Maximum road speed: 61.5km/hour
Maximum road range: 600km
Gradient: 60%
Vertical obstacle: 0.8m
Trench: 2.5m

Armour: Proof against small arms and shell splinters

ARMAMENT:
1x 23mm 2A14 cannon (600 rounds)
1x 7.62mm PKT MG (2,000 rounds)
1x AT-3 Sagger ATGM (1 + 3 missiles)

MLI-84 (ROMANIA)

The MLI-84 was very similar to the BMP-1, although it was larger and heavier than the Soviet vehicle. The most obvious difference was a 12.7mm anti-aircraft machine gun mounted at the right rear of the troop compartment. Where the BMP-1 had four rectangular roof hatches over the troop compartment, the MLI-84 had three. The right rear hatch was replaced with a circular hatch cover, with a 12.7mm DShKM anti-aircraft machine gun mounted on it.

The MLI-84 was fitted with an NBC system and night-vision equipment for the driver, gunner, and commander. It was fully amphibious, propelled in the water by its tracks.

SPECIFICATIONS: MLI-84

Crew: 2 + 9 passengers
Combat weight: 16,600kg
Length: 7.32m
Width: 3.15m
Height: 1.97m
Ground clearance: 0.4m
Maximum road speed: 70km/hour

ARMAMENT:
1x 73mm 2A28 gun (40 rounds)
1x 7.62mm PKT MG (2,000 rounds)

Dismounting from an MLI-84

1x AT-3 Sagger ATGM (1 + 4 missiles)
1x 12.7mm DShKM MG (500 rounds)

ARMOUR:
Hull front upper: 7mm @ 80° [Effective: 40mm]
Hull front lower: 19mm @ 57° [Effective: 35mm]
Hull side upper: 16mm @ 14° [Effective: 16mm]
Hull side lower: 18mm
Hull rear upper: 16mm @ 19° [Effective: 17mm]
Hull rear lower: 16mm @ 19° [Effective: 17mm]
Hull top: 6mm
Belly: 7mm
Turret front: 23mm @ 42° [Effective: 31mm]
Turret sides: 19mm @ 36° [Effective: 23mm]
Turret rear: 13mm @ 30° [Effective: 15mm]
Turret top: 6mm
Turret mantlet: 26-33mm

Armoured Personnel Carriers

Even after the introduction of the BMP series of infantry fighting vehicles in the late 1960s, the Soviet Union continued to produce and use armoured personnel carriers, since these were cheaper to produce and maintain than infantry fighting vehicles. The choice of wheels rather than tracks for many of the APC models made them even more cost-effective in terms of production, maintenance, and training. This, however, came at a cost of decreased off-road mobility.

BTR-40

The BTR-40 was the first mass-produced Soviet APC, and entered service in 1950, based on a lengthened GAZ-63 4x4 lorry chassis. The commander and driver sat in the front, with the eight infantrymen in the open-topped rear. Entry and exit were via two rear doors, and a tarpaulin was carried to provide protection against inclement weather. Three pintle mounts for 7.62mm SGMB machine guns were fitted on the front and sides of the troop compartment. There was no NBC protection.

In 1956, the BTR-40V added a central tyre pressure regulation system to improve off-road mobility. Later production vehicles had two or three firing ports in each side of the hull, and some vehicles had a 4,500kg capacity winch at the front. In 1957,

BTR-40

the BTR-40B was introduced. This had overhead armour for the troop compartment, but could only carry six infantrymen instead of eight.

An NBC reconnaissance variant, the BTR-40Kh, had equipment for setting marker poles with pennants into the ground while crossing contaminated areas. The BTR-40zhd, introduced in 1969, was a rail-scout variant. This was identical to the standard BTR-40, but with extra rail wheels that could be lowered for running on railway lines.

One other variant was produced for use by the East German army. This had a triple AT-3 Sagger launcher in the rear compartment, with overhead cover. This never entered front-line service, but was used as a training vehicle.

Specifications: BTR-40

Crew: 2 + 8 passengers
Combat weight: 5,300kg
Length: 5m
Width: 1.9m
Height: 1.75m
Ground clearance: 0.3m
Maximum road speed: 80km/hour
Maximum road range: 285km
Gradient: 60%
Vertical obstacle: 0.47m
Trench: 0.7m
Armament: 1-3x 7.62mm SGMB MG
Armour: 6-8mm

BTR-152

Production of the BTR-152 started in 1950, and it was accepted for service in the same year. The vehicle was based on a 6x6 lorry chassis (initially the ZIL-151, later the ZIL-157). Up to 17 men could be carried in the open-topped troop compartment, with entry and exit via two doors in the rear. A tarpaulin was carried for protection against inclement weather. The troop compartment had a total of eight firing ports, three on each side and two in the rear. There were three machine gun mounts - one at the front for a 7.62mm SGMB or 12.7mm DShKM machine gun, and one on each side for a 7.62mm SGMB machine gun. There was no NBC protection.

In 1955, the BTR-152V entered service. This was basically the same as the earlier model, but had a central tyre pressure regulation system to improve cross-country performance. In 1962, the BTR-152V1 added a front-mounted winch with a

BTR-152K

capacity of 5,000kg. The BTR-152V3 added infra-red driving lights. The BTR-152K had all the improvements included in the BTR-152V3, plus overhead armour with two roof hatches.

The command variant was designated BTR-152U. It was based on a BTR-152V1 or BTR-152V3, with overhead armour and a higher superstructure to allow command staff to stand upright. Windows were provided (two on the left, one each on the right and rear). Stowage racks were fitted to the roof, and the vehicle usually towed a trailer to carry extra equipment, such as a generator.

Specifications: BTR-152V1

Crew: 2 + 17 passengers
Combat weight: 8,950kg
Length: 6.83m
Width: 2.32m

Height: 2.05m
Ground clearance: 0.3m
Maximum road speed: 75km/hour
Maximum road range: 780km
Gradient: 55%
Vertical obstacle: 0.6m
Trench: 0.69m
Armament: 1x 7.62mm SGMB or 12.7mm DShKM MG

ARMOUR:
Front: 13.5mm @ 35° [Effective: 16mm]
Side: 9mm
Rear: 9mm @ 7° [Effective: 9.1mm]
Top (BTR-152K): 6mm
Belly: 4mm

BTR-50P

The BTR-50P entered production in 1954, based on the same chassis as the PT-76 light tank. It was the standard APC in tank divisions, until it was eventually replaced by the BMP series of infantry fighting vehicles. As late as 1990, there were still twenty-one BTR-50s in service with the Soviet army, all in Central Europe.

The BTR-50P was of all-welded construction, with the driver and commander seated at the front, an open-topped troop compartment for 20 infantrymen in the centre, and the engine at the rear. A pintle mount for a 7.62mm SGMB machine gun was fitted to the front of the troop compartment. There were ramps at the rear of the hull to allow an anti-tank gun or light field gun to be pulled onto the rear deck. The gun could be fired from the rear deck, even while the vehicle was swimming. The BTR-50P was fully amphibious, being propelled in the water by a pair of

BTR-50P

water jets. It had a searchlight, which could be white light or infra-red.

The BTR-50PA was a BTR-50P with the rear ramps removed, and a 14.5mm KPVT machine gun mounted over the commander's position. The BTR-50PK added overhead armour for the troop compartment, and NBC protection. Entry and exit were via roof hatches, and there were firing ports on both sides. The BTR-50PK retained the pintle mount for a 7.62mm SGMB machine gun.

The BTR-50PU was the command variant of the BTR-50. It had overhead armour and seats for four radio operators and four command staff, in addition to the two-person vehicle crew (driver and commander). It had a collapsible map table, a small table for the commander, hammocks, and thermal insulation. In addition to extra radio equipment and associated aerials, it carried four field telephones, a 10-line field telephone switchboard, and four 600m reels of telephone wire.

Specifications: BTR-50PK

Crew: 2 + 20 passengers
Combat weight: 14,200kg
Length: 7.08m
Width: 3.14m
Height: 1.97m
Ground clearance: 0.37m
Maximum road speed: 44km/hour
Maximum road range: 400km
Gradient: 70%
Vertical obstacle: 1.1m
Trench: 2.8m
Armament: 1x 7.62mm SGMB MG (1,250 rounds)
Armour: 6-10mm

BTR-60P

Following a competition between two design bureaus for a new wheeled APC to replace the BTR-152, the BTR-60P was accepted for service in 1960, for use in motor rifle divisions.

The BTR-60P was of all-welded construction, with the driver and commander seated at the front, an open-topped troop compartment in the centre, and a pair of petrol engines at the rear. A pintle mount for a 7.62mm SGMB or PK machine gun was fitted to the front of the troop compartment. Some vehicles had a 12.7mm DShKM machine gun fitted. There were mounts for 7.62mm SGMB or PK machine guns on the sides of the troop compartment. The BTR-60P was fully amphibious, being propelled in the water by a single water jet. All eight wheels were driven, and the first four were used for steering, which was power assisted. A central tyre pressure regulation system, infra-red night-vision equipment, and a front-mounted 4,500kg capacity

BTR-60PB

winch were fitted. The maximum troop capacity was 16, though normally only 12 were carried.

The BTR-60PA (sometimes referred to as the BTR-60PK), which entered service in 1963, added overhead armour and NBC protection. The roof had a large rectangular hatch at the front, with pintle mounts for machine guns to the front and sides of this hatch. Three firing ports were fitted on either side of the troop compartment. Entry and exit were via roof hatches; there were no side doors or hatches.

The BTR-60PA1 added a small one-man machine gun turret to the BTR-60PA, identical to the one fitted to the BRDM-2. This turret mounted a 14.5mm KPVT machine gun and a co-axial 7.62mm PKT machine gun. Gun elevation and turret traverse were both manual. This was closely followed by the BTR-60PB, which added other improvements, such as roof-mounted periscopes for the driver and commander, vision blocks in the troop compartment, and side hatches for improved entry and exit from the troop compartment. The addition of the turret reduced troop capacity to 14, though normally only eight infantrymen were carried.

There were several command variants of the BTR-60. The BTR-60PBK was used by company commanders, and was a BTR-60PB with additional radios. The BTR-60PU was a command variant of the BTR-60P, with a tarpaulin, map boards, and extra radios. The BTR-60PAU was a command version of the BTR-60PA, with a 10m-high aerial for use when stationary, a "clothes rail" aerial, and a generator. The BTR-60PU-12 was also based on the BTR-60PA, and operated with air-defence units. The BTR-60 ACRV was a command and observation post vehicle, which served with towed artillery batteries and battalions.

Specifications: BTR-60PB

Crew: 2 + 14 passengers (usually only eight passengers were carried)
Combat weight: 10,300kg
Length: 7.56m
Width: 2.83m
Height: 2.31m
Ground clearance: 0.48m
Maximum road speed: 80km/hour
Maximum road range: 500km
Gradient: 60%
Vertical obstacle: 0.4m
Trench: 2m
Armour: 5-9mm

Armament:
1x 14.5mm KPVT machine gun (500 rounds)
1x 7.62mm PKT machine gun (2,000 rounds)

BTR-70

The BTR-70 entered production in 1972, though it was not seen in public until 1980. Its design was similar to the BTR-60PB, but with various improvements. The armour was slightly thicker, and the front of the vehicle was redesigned to provide more protection to the front wheels. The layout was the same as the BTR-60PB, and the same turret was fitted, but two small doors were added to the sides of the troop compartment for safer entry and exit. Internal stowage for an RPG-7 light anti-tank weapon and two AGS-17 automatic grenade launchers were included. The front winch had a capacity of 6,000kg, an increase over that fitted to the BTR-60PB. Like the BTR-60PB, the BTR-70 was fitted with a central tyre pressure regulation system, infra-red night-vision equipment, and NBC protection. The BTR-70 was fully amphibious, propelled in the water by a single water jet.

Combat experience in Afghanistan led to the introduction of an improved version, the BTR-70M. This had the same turret as the BTR-80, with a higher elevation for the weapons, and six smoke grenade launchers at the rear. This model also added brackets to the sides of the hull for additional armour, and two extra firing ports between the hull sides and roof to allow embarked infantry to engage targets at high angles. In Afghanistan, some vehicles were spotted with 30mm AGS-17 automatic grenade launchers mounted on the roof, behind the driver's and commander's hatches. This was in addition to the standard turret.

An NBC reconnaissance version, the BTR-70Kh, had extra equipment for detecting contamination and marking areas. A command variant, the BTR-70KShM, had extra radio equipment.

BTR-70

SPW-70CH

This was a variant developed for the East German army by the Soviet Union. It mounted a bank of 81mm smoke grenade launchers on the back of the turret, in a similar arrangement to the BTR-80.

SPECIFICATIONS: BTR-70

Crew: 2 + 9 passengers
Combat weight: 11,500kg
Length: 7.54m
Width: 2.8m
Height: 2.32m
Ground clearance: 0.48m
Maximum road speed: 80km/hour
Maximum road range: 450km
Gradient: 60%

Vertical obstacle: 0.5m
Trench: 2m
Armour: 5-10mm

ARMAMENT:
1x 14.5mm KPVT machine gun (500 rounds)
1x 7.62mm PKT machine gun (2,000 rounds)

BTR-80

The BTR-80 was a further progression of the BTR-60PB and BTR-70, and was largely similar to the earlier vehicles. Production began in 1984, and in 1988, units started to be delivered to the naval infantry to replace their BTR-60PBs. The BTR-80 replaced the twin petrol engines of the earlier vehicles with a single V8 diesel engine, which improved speed, range, and survivability.

The BTR-80 turret was an improvement on the earlier models. Elevation was increased from +30° to +60°, a new sight was fitted, and it had a bank of six smoke grenade dischargers at the rear. This new turret was designed to allow engagement of helicopters and targets on high ground. Compared to earlier vehicles, the BTR-80 was better able to withstand punishment. Experience in Afghanistan showed that anti-tank mines would usually only damage one wheel, and that the vehicle could continue to be driven on the other seven wheels.

The troop compartment had larger doors between the second and third axles, further improving ease of entry and exit for the vehicle's seven infantry. There were three firing ports in the side of the hull, angled forward. The front two ports were for use with the 7.62mm PK machine gun, while the others were for use with AKMS or AK-74 assault rifles. Each of the two roof hatches also had a firing port. The BTR-80 normally carried an AGS-17

BTR-80

automatic grenade launcher and a gripstock for a man-portable SAM system (SA-14 Gremlin, SA-16 Gimlet or SA-18 Grouse), with two missiles.

The BTR-80 had a front winch with a capacity of 6,000kg (which could be increased to 12,000kg with the aid of a pulley). It had a central tyre pressure regulation system, infra-red night-vision equipment, and NBC protection, including chemical and radiological reconnaissance devices. It was fully amphibious, propelled in the water by a single water jet.

SPECIFICATIONS: BTR-80

Crew: 2 + 10 passengers
Combat weight: 13,600kg
Length: 7.65m
Width: 2.9m
Height: 2.41m
Ground clearance: 0.48m

Maximum road speed: 90km/hour
Maximum road range: 600km
Gradient: 60%
Vertical obstacle: 0.5m
Trench: 2m
Armour: Proof against 12.7mm AP rounds

ARMAMENT:
1x 14.5mm KPVT machine gun (500 rounds)
1x 7.62mm PKT machine gun (2,000 rounds)

BTR-D

The BTR-D was based on a lengthened BMD-1 chassis, and was accepted for service in 1974 for use with the airborne forces. Like the BMD-1, it had a welded aluminium hull with front and side firing ports. The driver sat in the centre of the vehicle at the front, with an infantryman on either side of him operating the two 7.62mm PKT machine guns. A further ten infantrymen could be carried in the troop compartment to the rear, entering and exiting via a pair of rear doors. Four smoke grenade dischargers were fitted, two on each side of the hull. Some vehicles had a 30mm AGS-17 automatic grenade launcher fitted on a pintle mount. The BTR-D had NBC protection and was fully amphibious.

Two command variants were made. The BMD-KShM had a large "clothes rail" aerial around the superstructure, extra radios, no firing ports, and no smoke grenade dischargers. The BMD-1E was similar, but had a large telescopic aerial instead of the "clothes rail" aerial.

BTR-D prepared for parachute drop

Specifications: BTR-D

Crew: 1 + 12 passengers
Combat weight: 8,000kg
Length: 5.89m
Width: 2.63m
Height: 1.67m
Ground clearance: 0.1-0.45m
Maximum road speed: 60km/hour
Maximum road range: 500km
Armament: 2x 7.62mm PKT machine guns

Armour:
Hull front upper: 15mm @ 78° [Effective: 72mm]
Hull front lower: 15mm @ 50° [Effective: 23mm]
Hull side: 10mm
Hull rear: 10mm

MT-LB

The MT-LB entered production in the early 1970s, and was used in various roles, including artillery prime mover and cargo carrier, as well as armoured personnel carrier.

The hull was made of welded steel armour, with the two-man crew seated at the front, engine immediately behind the crew, and troop/cargo compartment at the rear. There were twin doors at the rear of the vehicle. The driver sat to the left, with the commander (who also operated the small machine gun turret) to his right. The manually operated turret mounted a single 7.62mm PKT machine gun. Firing ports were fitted on each side of the rear compartment and in each of the rear doors.

The MT-LB was amphibious, propelled in the water by its tracks. It had NBC protection, a white/infra-red searchlight, and an infra-red periscope for the driver. It could carry up to 11 men or 6,500kg of cargo in the rear compartment, or tow a trailer or weapon weighing up to 6,500kg.

The SNAR-10 was an MT-LB with a Big Fred radar on a rotating mount at the rear of the vehicle. Initially thought by NATO to be an artillery radar location system, it was actually a battlefield surveillance radar. In 1982 the SNAR-10M was introduced. It was not amphibious, but retained the machine gun turret and NBC protection. In addition, it had extra communications equipment, an auxiliary power unit, a heater, and a navigation system.

The MT-LBV variant had wider tracks (565mm instead of the usual 350mm). The wider tracks reduced ground pressure from 0.46kg/cm2 to 0.28kg/cm2, and so this model was often used on snow and swampy ground. It was sometimes fitted with a 12.7mm NSVT machine gun in the turret instead of the usual 7.62mm PKT machine gun.

MT-LB

The MT-LB AT artillery tractor had ammunition stowage racks on the left side of the rear compartment. The ADZM was an engineer variant used in airborne brigades. This had a bulldozer blade, and an arm with a bucket was mounted on the roof. The MT-LBU was a command variant, with extra radios, a generator, and a navigation system. An ambulance variant had stretchers in the rear compartment.

The Poles made a variant fitted with the WAT turret (as fitted on the OT-64 and some OT-62 variants). This turret had a 14.5mm KPVT and a 7.62mm PKT machine gun.

SPECIFICATIONS: MT-LB

Crew: 2 + 11 passengers
Combat weight: 11,900kg
Maximum payload: 2,000kg
Maximum towed load: 6,500kg
Length: 6.45m

Width: 2.86m
Height: 1.87m
Ground clearance: 0.4m
Maximum road speed: 62km/hour
Maximum road range: 500km
Gradient: 60%
Vertical obstacle: 0.6m
Trench: 2.41m
Armament: 1x 7.62mm PKT machine gun (2,500 rounds)
Armour: 4-10mm

OT-810 (CZECHOSLOVAKIA)

During the Second World War, the Skoda plant in Pilsen manufactured the German Sdkfz 251 half-tracked armoured personnel carrier. Production continued after the war ended, but was stopped when the communists took power. In the mid-1950s the Czech army was looking for an armoured personnel carrier to use instead of the Soviet BTR-152. A modified version of the Sdkfz 251, designed by Tatra, was selected. The modifications included an armoured roof and a new Tatra 120hp diesel engine to replace the original petrol engine.

The hull was made of welded steel, with the engine at the front. The commander and driver were seated behind the engine, in the centre of the vehicle, with the driver on the left. The commander was provided with a pintle-mounted 7.62mm machine gun. Both commander and driver had to access their positions via the troop compartment.

The troop compartment was at the rear, with a pair of doors at the back of the vehicle for entry and exit. Two roof hatches opened to either side of the hull. The OT-810 had no NBC capability, night-vision equipment, or amphibious capability. The

M59A mounted on OT-810

vehicle wasn't a great success, and was unpopular with the troops, earning the nickname "Hitler's Revenge".

The OT-810 was often used as a tow vehicle for the 82mm M59A recoilless gun. After the OT-64 had replaced the OT-810 in the APC role, OT-810s were modified to mount the M59A as a self-propelled gun system. In this variant, the M59A was mounted in the troop compartment, with armoured shields to the front and sides. These could be folded down when the gun was in use. The M59A had a traverse of 90° when mounted in this way, an elevation of 25°, and a depression of 5°. The troop compartment's rear doors were replaced with a single hatch, which lowered to a horizontal position, giving more room for the gun crew.

The M59A could be removed and used from a ground mount with a traverse of 360°. HEAT and HE ammunition were carried, and there were sights for both indirect and direct fire. A spotting rifle was fitted to help with aiming in the direct fire role.

Specifications: OT-810

Crew: 2 + 10 passengers
Combat weight: 8,500kg
Length: 5.8m
Width: 2.1m
Height: 1.75m
Ground clearance: 0.3m
Maximum road speed: 53km/hour
Maximum road range: 320km
Gradient: 50%
Vertical obstacle: 0.26m
Trench: 1.98m
Armament: 1x 7.62mm machine gun

Armour:
Hull front: 12mm
Hull side: 7mm

OT-62 (Czechoslovakia/Poland)

The OT-62 was jointly developed by Czechoslovakia and Poland, and was similar to the BTR-50P, the main physical difference being a pair of cylindrical bays projecting to the front. In comparison to the Soviet vehicle, the OT-62 had a more powerful engine, overhead armour, and NBC protection. It entered Czech service in 1964, and Polish service (where it was known as the TOPAS) in 1966. Both countries deployed the tracked OT-62 with tank divisions, while motor rifle divisions were equipped with the wheeled OT-64.

OT-62B. The recoilless gun is not fitted, but the mountings are visible

The OT-62 had an all-welded hull, with the crew compartment at the front and the engine at the rear. The driver sat in the middle, with a single-piece hatch cover fitted with an integral vision block. The commander sat in the left projecting bay, and was provided with a cupola that could be traversed by hand through a full 360°. Both projecting bays at the front of the vehicle were fitted with observation periscopes.

Access to the troop compartment was by a pair of large doors, one on each side of the vehicle. Each door had an observation/firing port, and each side had an additional port forward of the door. Two large rectangular hatches were fitted in the roof of the troop compartment.

The engine was behind the troop compartment, with access panels in the roof for maintenance. An automatic fire-suppression system was fitted in the engine compartment, which could be manually activated if required.

The OT-62 was fully amphibious, propelled in the water by a pair of water jets at the rear of the hull. Before entering the water, bilge pumps were switched on and a trim vane erected at the front. An over-pressure NBC system was fitted, and an infra-red driving light was mounted at the front right of the vehicle. The initial version, the OT-62A, was unarmed, although an M59A recoilless gun could be carried on, and fired from, the rear deck.

The OT-62B was only used by the Czech army, and was fitted with the same manually-operated turret as the OT-65A, mounted on top of the right bay. This had a 7.62mm M59T machine gun, with an 82mm T-21 recoilless gun mounted externally on the right side. An infra-red searchlight was mounted to the right of the recoilless gun. The T-21 could be aimed and fired from inside the turret, but could only be reloaded from outside. It had a maximum range of 2,500m, although the effective range was significantly less, at 300m to 450m. The 82mm HEAT projectile could penetrate up to 230mm of armour.

The TOPAS-2AP (sometimes referred to as the OT-62C) was only used by the Polish army. This mounted the same small turret as the OT-64C in the centre of the hull, reducing the space in the troop compartment. This turret was similar to the one fitted on the Soviet BTR-60PB and BRDM-2, mounting a 14.5mm KPVT and 7.62mm PKT machine gun. The TOPAS-2AP was often used to carry a pair of 82mm mortars and their four-man crews.

SPECIFICATIONS: OT-62B (TOPAS-2AP IN BRACKETS)

Crew: 2 + 18 passengers (2 + 12 passengers)
Combat weight: 15,000kg (16,390kg)
Length: 7.08m (7m)
Width: 3.14m (3.23m)
Height: 2.23m (2.73m)

Ground clearance: 0.37m (0.43m)
Maximum road speed: 58km/hour (60km/hour)
Maximum road range: 460km (570km)
Gradient: 65%
Vertical obstacle: 1.1m
Trench: 2.8m

Armament (OT-62B):
1x 7.62mm M59T machine gun (1,250 rounds)
1x 82mm T-21 recoilless gun (12 rounds)

Armament (TOPAS-2AP):
1x 14.5mm KPVT machine gun (500 rounds)
1x 7.62mm PKT machine gun (2,000 rounds)

Armour:
Hull front upper: 8mm @ 83° [Effective: 66mm]
Hull front lower: 10mm @ 53° [Effective: 17mm]
Hull side upper: 10mm
Hull side lower: 9mm
Hull rear upper: 7mm
Hull rear lower: 6mm @ 42° [Effective: 8mm]
Hull top: 7mm @ 86° [Effective: 100mm]
Belly: 6mm

OT-64/SKOT (Czechoslovakia/Poland)

Czechoslovakia and Poland began development of the OT-64 (SKOT in Poland) in 1959, and it entered service in 1964. The Czech company Tatra provided the chassis and automotive parts, many of which were the same as those used in the Tatra 813 series of lorries. FSC/Lubin of Poland provided the armoured body and weapon systems. It bore some resemblance to the Soviet BTR-60, though with notable differences.

OT-64C

The hull was welded steel, with the crew compartment at the front, the engine behind the crew, and the troop compartment at the rear. The driver sat on the left with the commander to his right, each with a side door and roof hatch. A searchlight was fitted to the roof between the hatches, and could be operated from inside the crew compartment.

Unlike the BTR-60, the OT-64 was powered by a single diesel engine. A pair of doors in the rear of the hull were the usual passenger entry/exit point, although there were also roof hatches, which could be locked in the vertical position if required. Firing ports were provided to the rear and sides, and the seats could be folded away to allow the vehicle to carry cargo instead of infantry.

Power steering was provided to the front four wheels, and all eight wheels had a tyre pressure regulation system. It was fully amphibious, with a pair of propellers at the rear of the hull providing propulsion in the water. A trim vane, which normally rested on the glacis, was erected before entering the water. An NBC protection system was also fitted, as well as a winch, and bilge pumps for use when swimming.

The original version was fully enclosed, with five roof hatches. Initially unarmed, it was later fitted with a 7.62mm machine gun on a pintle mount at the front of the troop compartment. Some models have been seen with a pair of AT-3 Sagger ATGMs mounted over the troop compartment.

The SKOT-2 was only used by Poland, and may have been a temporary measure pending delivery of the OT-64C. It had a square plinth with a 7.62mm or 12.7mm machine gun. The machine gun had a shield to provide the gunner with protection to the front.

The OT-64C (SKOT-2A) had an eight-sided plinth in the centre of the vehicle, and the five roof hatches over the troop compartment were reduced to four. A one-man, manually operated turret was mounted on the plinth. This turret was similar to that fitted on the Soviet BTR-60PB and BRDM-2, mounting a 14.5mm KPVT and 7.62mm PKT machine gun. Some vehicles had a pair of AT-3 Sagger missiles mounted on the turret, one on each side.

The SKOT-2AP was only used by Poland, and mounted a new turret with a curved top. It had the same armament as the OT-64C, but the weapons had an elevation of 89.5°, allowing them to be used against helicopters. Some turrets have been seen with a pair of AT-3 Sagger ATGMs fitted.

There were several command variants of the OT-64, with extra radios and aerials.

SPECIFICATIONS: OT-64C/SKOT-2A

Crew: 2 + 10 passengers
Combat weight: 14,500kg
Length: 7.44m
Width: 2.55m
Height: 2.71m
Ground clearance: 0.46m
Maximum road speed: 94km/hour
Maximum road range: 710km

Gradient: 60%
Vertical obstacle: 0.5m
Trench: 2m

Armament:
1x 14.5mm KPVT machine gun (500 rounds)
1x 7.62mm PKT machine gun (2,000 rounds)

Armour (max):
Hull: 10mm
Turret: 14mm

PSZH-IV (Hungary)

Initially, NATO mistakenly classified this vehicle as an amphibious scout car, and labelled it FÚG-66, then FÚG-70. Later, it was discovered to be an armoured personnel carrier. It was generally referred to in the West as the PSZH-IV, but the Hungarian designation was PSZH D-944.

The cross-country capability was not as good as the Soviet BTR series and Czech/Polish OT series, and it carried fewer passengers. Despite these shortcomings, it was adopted by the Hungarian army in preference to foreign imports.

The driver and commander sat at the front, each with a hatch and windscreen. The hatch covers were fitted with vision blocks for use when the hatches were closed. Each side of the vehicle had a two-piece door, four vision blocks, and two firing ports for the passengers. Six infantrymen could be carried in addition to the crew.

A small turret was fitted in the centre of the vehicle. It was similar to that on the BRDM-2, but not identical. The turret had a day periscope and a ventilator fan. The diesel engine was fitted behind the turret.

The PSZH-IV was fully amphibious. A trim board stowed on the glacis was erected before entering the water, where the vehicle was propelled by a pair of water jets at the rear of the hull. It was fitted with NBC protection, a powered winch, and a central tyre pressure regulation system. Night-vision equipment included infra-red driving lights and an infra-red searchlight mounted co-axially to the right of the main armament. Armament consisted of a 14.5mm KPVT machine gun with a 7.62mm PKT machine gun mounted co-axially.

Variants included a version without a turret, which was used for command, ambulance, and NBC reconnaissance. A second command version had a turret, but did not carry infantry. A turreted NBC reconnaissance version also existed, with similar equipment to the Soviet BRDM-2-RKha.

SPECIFICATIONS: PSZH-IV

Crew: 3 + 6 passengers
Combat weight: 7,600kg
Length: 5.7m
Width: 2.5m
Height: 2.31m
Ground clearance: 0.42m
Maximum road speed: 80km/hour
Maximum road range: 500km
Gradient: 60%
Vertical obstacle: 0.4m
Trench: 0.6m
Armour (max): 14mm

ARMAMENT:
1x 14.5mm KPVT machine gun (500 rounds)
1x 7.62mm PKT machine gun (2,000 rounds)

TAB-71 (Romania)

The TAB-71 was a licence-built copy of the BTR-60PB, and so was very similar to the Soviet vehicle. The central tyre pressure regulation system, winch, amphibious capability, and NBC protection remained. The engines were replaced with more powerful 140hp versions, leading to an increase in speed. A large hatch was added to each side in the centre, above the second/third road wheels.

The TAB-71M replaced the original turret with a new, locally-designed one. This had the same armament of 14.5mm KPVT and co-axial 7.62mm PKT, but added a day gunsight on the left side, with a distinctive protective cage.

A mortar carrier variant, the TAB-71AR, had no turret, and carried an 82mm mortar, fired through the open roof hatches. This variant had a PKMS machine gun fitted at the rear of the vehicle, operated by opening a roof hatch.

Specifications: TAB-71

Crew: 3 + 8 passengers
Combat weight: 11,000kg
Length: 7.22m
Width: 2.83m
Height: 2.7m
Ground clearance: 0.47m
Maximum road speed: 95km/hour
Maximum road range: 500km
Gradient: 60%
Vertical obstacle: 0.4m
Trench: 2m

TAB-71M

ARMAMENT:
1x 14.5mm KPVT machine gun (500 rounds)
1x 7.62mm PKT machine gun (2,000 rounds)

ARMOUR:
Hull: 9mm max
Turret: 7mm max

TAB-77 (ROMANIA)

This was a Romanian-designed copy of the Soviet BTR-70, with some differences. Designed in the 1970s, production started in 1978. The TAB-77 had a pair of diesel engines in place of the BTR-70's petrol engines. Internal layout was similar to the Soviet vehicle, and it had the same turret as the TAB-71. The commander was provided with a roof-mounted searchlight that could be operated from inside the vehicle.

Like the BTR-70, it was fully amphibious. Before entering the water, a trim vane was erected at the front and bilge pumps were switched on. This could be done by the driver from his seat. A single water jet provided propulsion in the water.

The TAB-77 had NBC protection, infra-red night-vision equipment, automatic fire detection and suppression systems,

TAB-77

power steering, central tyre pressure regulation, and an engine preheater. A 5,500kg capacity winch was fitted at the front.

SPECIFICATIONS: TAB-77

Crew: 2 + 9 passengers
Combat weight: 13,350kg
Length: 7.42m
Width: 2.95m
Height: 2.32m
Ground clearance: 0.53m
Maximum road speed: 83km/hour
Maximum road range: 550km
Gradient: 60%
Vertical obstacle: 0.5m
Trench: 2m
Armour: 5-10mm

ARMAMENT:
1x 14.5mm KPVT machine gun (600 rounds)
1x 7.62mm PKT machine gun (2,500 rounds)

MLVM Mountaineers Combat Vehicle (Romania)

The MLVM was specifically designed to carry seven men and its crew of two in mountainous terrain. It could also be used to carry logistical stores such as ammunition. Construction was of welded steel, with armour sufficient to provide protection against small arms and shell splinters.

The driver sat at the front left, and was provided with a roof hatch and three day periscopes, one of which could be replaced with a night-vision device. The commander, sitting behind the driver, also had a roof hatch and three day periscopes. One of the commander's periscopes could be raised for forward observation, and he had an infra-red searchlight.

A turret, the same design as that on the TAB-71M, was fitted in the centre, with the troop compartment to its rear. Troop compartment entry and exit was through a pair of roof hatches or a door in the rear of the vehicle. One passenger would man the turret, with six in the troop compartment, sat facing outwards, each with a firing port and periscope. Two firing ports and periscopes were also fitted in the rear door. The MLVM was amphibious, propelled in the water by its tracks.

Specifications: MLVM

Crew: 2 + 7 passengers
Combat weight: 9,000kg
Length: 5.85m
Width: 2.71m
Height: 1.95m
Ground clearance: 0.38m
Maximum road speed: 48km/hour
Maximum road range: 700km

Gradient: 60%

Vertical obstacle: 0.6m

Trench: 1.5m

Armour: Proof against small arms and shell splinters

ARMAMENT:

1x 14.5mm KPVT machine gun (600 rounds)

1x 7.62mm PKT machine gun (2,500 rounds)

Anti-Tank Vehicles

With the introduction of anti-tank guided missiles in the 1950s, most Soviet anti-tank vehicles switched to missile armament, the notable exception being vehicles intended for the airborne forces. The introduction of the BMD provided the airborne forces with useful anti-tank firepower, and so development of gun-armed tank destroyers stopped altogether.

There were rumours of a tank destroyer designated the IT-130, based on a T-62 tank chassis and armed with an 130mm gun. This was "revealed" to the West by a defector, the former GRU agent known as Viktor Suvorov (real name Vladimir Rezun). It was claimed to mount a 130mm gun in an armoured superstructure on a T-62 chassis. The claim was eventually discovered to be completely fictitious, although Suvorov's motive remains unknown. He may have been trying to spread disinformation, or simply trying to please his investigators.

A design for a self-propelled 130mm gun, the ISU-130, did exist. Development of this vehicle, which was fitted with an adapted 130mm naval gun, started toward the end of the Second World War, and was abandoned after the war ended. There were several problems with the design, and it did not enter production.

SU-100

The SU-100 entered service in 1944, and remained in production until 1953 in the Soviet Union, and 1956 in Czechoslovakia. The welded hull housed the fighting compartment at the front, with the engine at the rear. The driver sat at the front left, and had a large hatch that opened upwards, with vision blocks for use when closed up. The gunner was positioned behind the driver, and had a hatch with an observation periscope, in addition to the gun sight. The loader was stationed at the rear of the fighting compartment, and the commander was seated to the right of the gun. He had a cupola with a periscope that could be turned through 360°.

Four long-range fuel tanks could be fitted, two on each side. The SU-100 had no night-vision equipment, NBC protection, or amphibious capability. Armament was a 100mm D-10S gun, developed from a naval gun, which was mounted to the right of the centre line. Elevation and traverse were manual, and it was not fitted with a fume extractor or muzzle brake.

A follow-on vehicle was developed, based on the T-44 chassis. This was armed with a 100mm D-10T gun, with the engine at the front and the fighting compartment at the rear. It did not enter production. A command variant, with armament removed, was produced in small numbers. This had space for map boards, seats for command staff, and additional radios.

Specifications: SU-100

Crew: 4
Combat weight: 31.6 tonnes
Length: 6.19m (9.45m including gun)
Width: 3.05m
Height: 2.24m

SU-100

Ground clearance: 0.4m
Maximum road speed: 55km/hour
Maximum road range: 300km
Gradient: 60%
Vertical obstacle: 0.73m
Trench: 2.5m
Armament: 1x 100mm D-10S gun (34 rounds)

ARMOUR:
Hull front upper: 78mm @ 50° [Effective: 121mm]
Hull front lower: 45mm @ 60° [Effective: 90mm]
Hull sides upper: 45mm @ 20° [Effective: 48mm]
Hull sides lower: 45mm
Hull top: 18-22mm
Belly: 18-22mm
Hull rear: 47mm @ 50° [Effective: 73mm]
Mantlet: 75mm

SU-122-54

Design of the SU-122-54 (sometimes erroneously referred to as the IT-122, which was another invention of Suvorov's) began in 1949, and it was accepted for service in 1954. The unusual "-54" suffix was added to the designation to avoid confusion with the wartime SU-122 self-propelled howitzer. It was only in production for two years (1955-1956), and fewer than 100 vehicles were built.

The SU-122-54 was based on a T-54 chassis, with a D-49 122mm gun mounted in a superstructure situated at the front, and equipped with a double-baffle muzzle brake and fume extractor. Two KPVT 14.5mm machine guns were fitted: one co-axial with the main armament, one mounted on the loader's hatch for use against aircraft.

SPECIFICATIONS: SU-122-54/IT-122

Crew: 5
Combat weight: 36 tonnes
Length: 6m (9.97m including gun)
Width: 3.27m
Height: 2.06m
Ground clearance: 0.43m
Maximum road speed: 48km/hour
Maximum road range: 400km
Gradient: 58%
Vertical obstacle: 0.73m
Trench: 2.7m

ARMAMENT:
1x 122mm D-49 gun (35 rounds)
2x 14.5mm KPVT MG (600 rounds)

ARMOUR:
Front: 100mm @ 55° [Effective: 174mm]
Side: 80mm @ 17° [Effective: 84mm]
Top: 20mm
Belly: 20mm

ASU-57

The ASU-57 was specifically designed to be very light, for service with the airborne divisions. It entered service in 1950, initially carried under the wings in special aluminium containers. When larger transport aircraft were developed, it was carried inside, and parachuted from the rear door on a special pallet.

Initially made of steel, aluminium was later used, resulting in a significant decrease in weight. The engine and transmission were at the front of the vehicle, with the open-topped crew compartment at the rear. The driver and loader sat to the right of the gun. The commander/gunner sat to the left, with the fuel tank and ammunition behind him. More ammunition was held behind the loader's position. A tarpaulin was carried for use in inclement weather.

Armament consisted of a Ch-51 or Ch-51M 57mm gun. The Ch-51 was recognisable by the long, multi-slotted muzzle brake. The more common Ch-51M had a conventional double-baffle muzzle brake.

SPECIFICATIONS: ASU-57

Crew: 3
Combat weight: 3.4 tonnes
Length: 3.48m (with gun)
Width: 2.8m
Height: 1.18m

ASU-57 with Ch-51 gun

Maximum road speed: 45km/hour
Maximum road range: 250km
Armament: 1x 57mm Ch-51 or Ch-51M gun (30 rounds)
Armour: 6mm

ASU-85

Development of the ASU-85 started in the 1950s as a replacement for the ASU-57, and it entered production in 1960. The chassis was based on a heavily modified PT-76 chassis. The hull was all-welded, with the fighting compartment at the front and engine at the rear. The driver sat at the front of the vehicle on the right, with the commander behind him. The gunner and loader were both seated to the left of the main armament.

ASU-85

The main armament was a D-70 85mm gun with a co-axial 7.62mm SGMT machine gun. An infra-red searchlight was mounted over the main armament, moving in elevation and traverse with the gun. Later vehicles were fitted with a 12.7mm DShKM machine gun mounted on the roof, and some vehicles were fitted with smoke grenade dischargers at the rear of the hull, firing over the frontal arc.

The ASU-85 was air-portable, but because of the significant increase in weight compared to the ASU-57, could not be dropped by parachute. It had NBC protection for the crew, but was not amphibious. It was later replaced in service by the BMD-1.

Specifications: ASU-85

Crew: 4
Combat weight: 15.5 tonnes
Length: 6m (8.49m including gun)
Width: 2.8m
Height: 2.1m
Maximum road speed: 45km/hour
Maximum road range: 230km
Armour: 40-45mm

Armament:
1x 85mm D-70 gun (45 rounds)
1x 7.62mm SGMT MG (2,000 rounds)
1x 12.7mm DShKM MG (later vehicles)

2P26

The first Soviet anti-tank guided missile, the AT-1 Snapper, used manual command to line-of-sight guidance, with a wire link to transmit guidance commands to the missile. It was too large and heavy for a man-portable launcher, and so vehicular launchers were developed. The first of these, the 2P26, was a modified UAZ-69 light lorry and entered service in the late 1950s. It was sometimes referred to as the "Baby Carriage".

Four missiles were mounted on launch rails fitted behind the cab and covered with a canvas top. The launch rails pointed vertically upwards during transit, and were rotated to a near-horizontal position for firing. Two crew (driver and gunner) were seated in the cab. The gunner's seat faced to the rear, and both driver and gunner were provided with rear-facing sights. The guidance system could be deployed up to 30m away from the vehicle to allow remote firing.

2P26

SPECIFICATIONS: 2P26

Weight: 2.18 tonnes
Length: 3.85m
Width: 1.85m
Height: 2.03m
Maximum road speed: 90km/hour
Armament: 4x AT-1 missiles

SPECIFICATIONS: AT-1

Guidance: MCLOS (wire link)
Range: 500-2,000m
Length: 1.15m
Diameter: 136mm
Weight: 22.5kg
Warhead: 5.4kg HEAT
Penetration: 300mm

2P27

The 2P27 entered service in 1960, based on a BRDM-1 chassis. Three AT-1 missiles were mounted on retractable launch

2P27

rails. To fire, overhead covers were removed and placed on the side of the vehicle, a flap in the rear of the superstructure was opened, and the launch rails were raised. The guidance unit could be detached, allowing the gunner to be sited up to 50m away from the vehicle. The large size of the missile meant that on-board reloads could not be carried.

Specifications: BRDM-1

Crew: 5
Unloaded weight: 5,600kg
Length: 5.7m
Width: 2.25m
Height: 1.9m
Ground clearance: 0.315m
Maximum road speed: 80km/hour
Maximum road cruising range: 500km
Gradient: 60%

Vertical obstacle: 0.4m
Trench: 1.22m
Armament: 3x AT-1 missiles
Armour (max): 10mm

Specifications: AT-1

Guidance: MCLOS (wire link)
Range: 500–2,000m
Length: 1.15m
Diameter: 136mm
Weight: 22.5kg
Warhead: 5.4kg HEAT
Penetration: 300mm

2P32

In 1962, the 2P32 entered service. Like the 2P27, the 2P32 was based on the BRDM-1, but carried the AT-2 Swatter instead of the AT-1 Snapper. The smaller wingspan of the newer missile meant that four, rather than three, missiles were carried. As with the 2P27, no reload missiles were carried.

Specifications: BRDM-1

Crew: 5
Unloaded weight: 5,600kg
Length: 5.7m
Width: 2.25m
Height: 1.9m
Ground clearance: 0.315m
Maximum road speed: 80km/hour
Maximum road cruising range: 500km
Gradient: 60%

Vertical obstacle: 0.4m
Trench: 1.22m
Armament: 4x AT-2 missiles
Armour (max): 10mm

Specifications: AT-2

Guidance: MCLOS (radio link)
Range: 500-2,500m
Length: 1.16m
Diameter: 148mm
Weight: 27kg
Warhead: 5.4kg HEAT
Penetration: 500mm

9P110

In 1963, the 9P110 entered service, with six AT-3 Sagger anti-tank missiles mounted on a BRDM-1 chassis. It used a new mounting, which was raised as a whole to fire, without first removing the armoured cover. This significantly reduced the time required to prepare for firing.

The smaller size of the AT-3 missile allowed eight reload missiles to be carried inside the vehicle. The guidance unit could be removed from the vehicle and operated from up to 80m away, allowing the gunner to avoid return fire directed at the launch point.

Specifications: BRDM-1

Crew: 5
Unloaded weight: 5,600kg
Length: 5.7m
Width: 2.25m

Tanks and Combat Vehicles of the Warsaw Pact | 101

9P110

Height: 1.9m
Ground clearance: 0.315m
Maximum road speed: 80km/hour
Maximum road cruising range: 500km
Gradient: 60%
Vertical obstacle: 0.4m
Trench: 1.22m
Armament: 6x AT-3 missiles (plus eight reloads)
Armour (max): 10mm

SPECIFICATIONS: AT-3

Guidance: MCLOS (wire link)
Range: 500-3,000m
Length: 860mm
Diameter: 125mm

Weight: 10.9kg
Warhead: 2.6kg HEAT
Penetration: 200mm @ 60° (later warheads increase this to 520mm)

IT-1

The IT-1 was a missile-armed tank destroyer based on a T-62 chassis. It had a limited production run and was in service from 1968 to 1970. A low turret was fitted, which incorporated a pop-up launcher for the 3M7 Drakon anti-tank missile with 12 reload missiles in an autoloader. Three further missiles were carried, but had to be manually loaded. A 7.62mm PKT machine gun was mounted in the turret. The vehicle had a crew of three: driver, gunner, and commander.

The 3M7 system used SACLOS guidance, with a radio link to send guidance commands to the missile. Night-vision equipment was fitted, but was only useful up to a range of around 600m, severely limiting the useful range of the missile at night.

Specifications: IT-1 Vehicle

Crew: 3
Combat weight: 34.5 tonnes
Length: 6.63m
Width: 3.3m
Height: 2.2m
Ground clearance: 0.43m
Maximum road speed: 50km/hour
Maximum road range: 470km
Gradient: 60%
Vertical obstacle: 0.8m
Trench: 2.85m

IT-1

Armament:
1x 3M7 Drakon ATGM (plus 15 reloads)
1x 7.62mm PKT MG (2,000 rounds)

Armour:
Hull front upper: 102mm @ 60° [Effective: 204mm]
Hull front lower: 102mm @ 54° [Effective: 174mm]
Hull side upper: 79mm
Hull side lower: 15mm
Hull rear: 46mm
Hull top: 31mm
Belly: 20mm
Turret front: 206mm

Specifications: 3M7 Drakon

Guidance: SACLOS (radio link)
Range: 300-3,300m (300-600m at night)
Length: 1.24m

Diameter: 180mm
Weight: 54kg
Warhead: 5.8kg HEAT
Penetration: 250mm @ 60°

9P124

First seen in 1973, this was a BRDM-2 with the turret removed. Four AT-2 Swatter C missiles were carried on launch rails, attached to the underside of an armoured, retractable roof. The launch assembly was lowered into the vehicle for travelling, and raised for firing. The Swatter C used semi-automatic command to line-of-sight guidance, with an infra-red link to transmit guidance commands to the missile. Four reload missiles were carried within the vehicle.

SPECIFICATIONS: BRDM-2

Crew: 4
Combat weight: 7,000kg
Length: 5.75m
Width: 2.35m
Height: 2.31m
Ground clearance: 0.43m
Maximum road speed: 100km/hour
Maximum road range: 750km
Gradient: 60%
Vertical obstacle: 0.4m
Trench: 1.25m
Armament: 4x AT-2 missiles (plus four reloads)

ARMOUR:
Hull front upper: 5mm @ 80° [Effective: 29mm]
Hull front lower: 7mm @ 45° [Effective: 10mm]

Hull nose plate: 14mm @ 14° [Effective: 14mm]
Hull sides upper: 7mm @ 18° [Effective: 7.1mm]
Hull sides lower: 7mm
Hull rear: 7mm
Hull top: 7mm
Belly: 2-3mm

Specifications: AT-2C

Guidance: SACLOS (radio link)
Range: 500-4,000m
Length: 1.16m
Diameter: 148mm
Weight: 29kg
Warhead: 5.4kg HEAT
Penetration: 500mm

9P122

This was a modified BRDM-2, similar to the 9P124. It carried six AT-3 Sagger missiles on launch rails under an armoured, retractable roof. The launch assembly was normally lowered into the vehicle, and was raised for firing. The AT-3 used manual command to line-of-sight guidance.

As well as launching missiles from within the vehicle, they could be launched remotely, from up to 80m away, using a separate sight. Eight reload missiles were carried, and could be loaded while the launch platform was inside the vehicle.

A later version, the 9P133, replaced the original version of the AT-3 missile with the AT-3C, which used the simpler and more accurate semi-automatic command to line-of-sight guidance. The vehicle had a larger sight, and was identifiable by an extra small window on the front.

Specifications: BRDM-2

Crew: 4
Combat weight: 7,000kg
Length: 5.75m
Width: 2.35m
Height: 2.31m
Ground clearance: 0.43m
Maximum road speed: 100km/hour
Maximum road range: 750km
Gradient: 60%
Vertical obstacle: 0.4m
Trench: 1.25m
Armament: 6x AT-3 missiles (plus eight reloads)

Armour:
Hull front upper: 5mm @ 80° [Effective: 29mm]
Hull front lower: 7mm @ 45° [Effective: 10mm]
Hull nose plate: 14mm @ 14° [Effective: 14mm]
Hull sides upper: 7mm @ 18° [Effective: 7.1mm]
Hull sides lower: 7mm
Hull rear: 7mm
Hull top: 7mm
Belly: 2-3mm

Specifications: AT-3 (AT-3C in brackets)

Guidance: MCLOS (wire link) (SACLOS, wire link)
Range: 500-3,000m
Length: 860mm
Diameter: 125mm
Weight: 10.9kg (11.4kg)
Warhead: 2.6kg HEAT
Penetration: 200mm @ 60° (520mm)

9P148

Initially wrongly identified in the West as the BRDM-3, this was a BRDM-2 with the turret removed and replaced with a mounting for five AT-5 Spandrel missiles. The mounting folded down for travelling, but did not retract into the vehicle. Missiles were reloaded via a hatch behind the launcher.

The missile sight was located in the front right of the vehicle. Ten AT-5 reload missiles were carried within the hull. The launcher could mount and fire AT-4 Spigot missiles as well as AT-5 Spandrel, and it was occasionally spotted with AT-4 missiles in the outer two mounts. In this case, seven AT-5 and eight AT-4 reload missiles were carried within the hull.

SPECIFICATIONS: BRDM-2

Crew: 4
Combat weight: 7,000kg
Length: 5.75m
Width: 2.35m
Height: 2.31m
Ground clearance: 0.43m
Maximum road speed: 100km/hour
Maximum road range: 750km
Gradient: 60%
Vertical obstacle: 0.4m
Trench: 1.25m
Armament: 10x AT-5 missiles (plus ten reloads) or 3x AT-5 and 2x AT-4 missiles (plus seven AT-5 and eight AT-4 reloads)

ARMOUR:
Hull front upper: 5mm @ 80° [Effective: 29mm]
Hull front lower: 7mm @ 45° [Effective: 10mm]
Hull nose plate: 14mm @ 14° [Effective: 14mm]

9P148

Hull sides upper: 7mm @ 18° [Effective: 7.1mm]
Hull sides lower: 7mm
Hull rear: 7mm
Hull top: 7mm
Belly: 2-3mm

SPECIFICATIONS: AT-4

Guidance: SACLOS (wire link)
Range: 70-2,000m
Length: 1.1m
Diameter: 120mm
Weight: 11.5kg
Warhead: HEAT
Penetration: 400mm @ 0°, 230mm @ 60°

SPECIFICATIONS: AT-5 (AT-5B IN BRACKETS)

Guidance: SACLOS (wire link)
Range: 75-4,000m

Length: 1.3m
Diameter: 135mm
Weight: 25.2kg (26.5kg)
Warhead: HEAT (Tandem HEAT)
Penetration: 600mm (750–800mm)

9P149

In 1990, it was announced that a new anti-tank vehicle, mounting an AT-6 Spiral launcher on an MT-LB chassis, had been deployed. The AT-6 used semi-automatic command to line-of-sight guidance, with a radio link to send guidance commands to the missile. The guidance system included ECCM (electronic counter-counter measures).

When the launcher was retracted, the vehicle was almost identical in appearance to a standard MT-LB, but the machine gun turret was replaced with a large sight at the front of the hull. The launcher, mounting a single missile, was retracted under armour for transport and loading, and raised for firing. A total of 12 missiles were carried in an autoloader. The system had a limited anti-aircraft capability, allowing it to engage attack helicopters.

The 9P149 retained the NBC protection and amphibious capability of the standard MT-LB. In the water, it was propelled by its tracks.

SPECIFICATIONS: MT-LB

Crew: 2 + 11 passengers
Combat weight: 11,900kg
Maximum payload: 2,000kg
Maximum towed load: 6,500kg
Length: 6.45m

9P149

Width: 2.86m
Height: 1.87m
Ground clearance: 0.4m
Maximum road speed: 62km/hour
Maximum road range: 500km
Gradient: 60%
Vertical obstacle: 0.6m
Trench: 2.41m
Armament: 1x AT-6 missile (plus twelve reloads)
Armour: 4-10mm

Specifications: AT-6

Guidance: SACLOS (radio link)
Range: 400-5,000m
Length: 1.83m
Diameter: 130mm
Weight: 48.5kg
Warhead: 5.3kg HEAT
Penetration: 560mm

Reconnaissance Vehicles

Although specialised reconnaissance vehicles are detailed in this chapter, it should be noted that the Warsaw Pact armies often fielded standard vehicles such as main battle tanks and IFVs alongside specialised vehicles in reconnaissance units.

BRDM-1

The BRDM-1 was accepted for service in 1957, and entered production in the same year. Initially it had an open-topped roof, but an enclosed roof was added in 1958 and this became the standard production model.

The hull was welded steel, with the engine at the front. The driver was seated on the left, with the commander to his right and the crew compartment behind them. There were two large hatches in the forward part of the roof. The BRDM-1 had four main wheels, all of which were driven. There were an additional four small wheels between the two main axles, which could be lowered by the driver for improved off-road and ditch-crossing performance. The vehicle was fully amphibious, propelled in the water by a single water jet. It did not have NBC protection, though it did have systems for detecting chemical warfare agents and nuclear contamination.

BRDM-1 with extra wheels lowered

Usual armament was a 7.62mm SGMB machine gun on a pintle mount at the front of the roof. Some vehicles were observed with a 12.7mm DShKM machine gun at the front, and a 7.62mm SGMB machine gun at the rear. There were two firing ports on each side of the hull, and two more at the rear.

The BRDM-1-RKhb NBC reconnaissance vehicle was a variant on the standard BRDM-1. This vehicle had NBC protection, and additional chemical sensors and nuclear contamination detectors. It also had a variety of alarm systems for warning nearby troops, including two rectangular racks containing marker poles with pennants.

SPECIFICATIONS: BRDM-1

Crew: 5
Unloaded weight: 5,600kg
Length: 5.7m
Width: 2.25m

Height: 1.9m
Ground clearance: 0.315m
Maximum road speed: 80km/hour
Maximum road cruising range: 500km
Gradient: 60%
Vertical obstacle: 0.4m
Trench: 1.22m
Armament: 1 × 7.62mm SGMB MG (1,250 rounds)
Armour (max): 10mm

BRDM-2

The BRDM-2 entered service during the 1960s. Based on the BRDM-1, it added a small turret and a more powerful engine, mounted at the rear instead of the front.

Like the BRDM-1, the armour was welded steel. The driver sat at the front left of the vehicle and the commander at the front right. There were roof hatches above the driver and commander for entry and exit. Immediately to the rear of these hatches was a small, manually operated, one-man turret. This had a 14.5mm KPVT machine gun with a co-axial 7.62mm PKT machine gun. A telescopic sight was provided for the main armament. Each side of the hull had a single firing port.

The BRDM-2 had four main wheels, all of which were driven. There were an additional four small wheels between the two main axles, which could be lowered by the driver for improved off-road and ditch-crossing performance. A central tyre pressure regulation system was fitted to further improve off-road performance.

The BRDM-2 was fitted with NBC protection, and was fully amphibious, propelled in the water by a single water jet at the rear of the hull. It had infra-red driving lights, an infra-red

BRDM-2s in convoy

searchlight, and a 4,000kg-capacity winch at the front of the hull.

The BRDM-2-RKha NBC reconnaissance vehicle was a variant on the standard BRDM-2. This vehicle had additional chemical sensors and nuclear contamination detectors. It also had a variety of alarm systems for warning nearby troops, including two rectangular racks containing marker poles with pennants. The later BRDM-2-RKhb replaced the 14.5mm KPVT with a second 7.62mm PKT, and had improved sensors.

SPECIFICATIONS: BRDM-2

Crew: 4
Combat weight: 7,000kg
Length: 5.75m
Width: 2.35m
Height: 2.31m
Ground clearance: 0.43m

Maximum road speed: 100km/hour
Maximum road range: 750km
Gradient: 60%
Vertical obstacle: 0.4m
Trench: 1.25m

Armament:
1x 14.5mm KPVT MG (500 rounds)
1x 7.62mm PKT MG (2,000 rounds)

Armour:
Hull front upper: 5mm @ 80° [Effective: 29mm]
Hull front lower: 7mm @ 45° [Effective: 10mm]
Hull nose plate: 14mm @ 14° [Effective: 14mm]
Hull sides upper: 7mm @ 18° [Effective: 7.1mm]
Hull sides lower: 7mm
Hull rear: 7mm
Hull top: 7mm
Belly: 2-3mm
Turret front: 7mm @ 43° [Effective: 10mm]
Turret sides: 7mm @ 36° [Effective: 9mm]
Turret rear: 7mm @ 36° [Effective: 9mm]
Turret top: 7mm

BRM

The BRM was accepted for service in 1972. It was based on the BMP-1, but had a larger, two-man turret and two roof hatches to the rear instead of the BMP-1's four. It was armed with a 73mm 2A28 smoothbore gun and co-axial 7.62mm PKT machine gun. Unlike the BMP-1, there was no ATGM launcher or autoloader. Some vehicles had a bank of six smoke grenade launchers at the rear of the turret, firing over the turret to the front.

BRM

The BRM had a laser rangefinder and a Tall Mike ground surveillance radar. The radar was normally kept in the turret and was elevated above the turret roof when required. It had additional navigation and radio equipment, compared to the BMP-1. The BRM had a crew of six: the driver and navigator in the front hull, the commander and gunner in the turret, and a pair of observers in the rear hull.

SPECIFICATIONS: BRM

Crew: 6
Combat weight: 12,500kg
Length: 6.75m
Width: 2.97m
Height: 1.98m
Ground clearance: 0.43m
Maximum road speed: 70km/hour
Maximum road range: 500km

Gradient: 60%
Vertical obstacle: 0.8m
Trench: 2.2m
Armour (max): 10mm

Armament:
1x 73mm 2A28 gun (20 rounds)
1x 7.62mm PKT MG (2,000 rounds)

BRM-23 (Bulgaria)

The BRM-23 was a development of the BMP-23, modified for reconnaissance missions up to 100km ahead of the main force. It retained the armament of the IFV version, but only had three firing ports (two on the right, one on the left). It had a five-man crew: two in the front hull, two in the turret, and one in the rear.

It carried a range of specialised equipment for its reconnaissance role, including a handheld laser rangefinder with a range of 9km, and a handheld passive night-vision device. Both of these could be mounted on tripods for greater stability if required. A land navigation system, artillery aiming circle, man-portable mine detector, and radiation and chemical detectors were also carried, as well as extra radios. A large frame aerial was carried. When erected at the rear of the hull, it extended the range of the RM-130M radio to around 120km.

Like the BMP-23, it was fully amphibious, powered in the water by its tracks, and had NBC protection for the crew.

Specifications: BRM-23

Crew: 5
Combat weight: 14,800kg
Length: 7.23m
Width: 3.01m

Height: 2.53m
Ground clearance: 0.4m
Maximum road speed: 61.5km/hour
Maximum road range: 500km
Gradient: 60%
Vertical obstacle: 0.8m
Trench: 2.5m

ARMAMENT:
1x 23mm 2A14 cannon (600 rounds)
1x 7.62mm PKT MG (2,000 rounds)
1x AT-3 Sagger ATGM (1 + 3 missiles)

FÚG (HUNGARY)

The Hungarian FÚG served a similar purpose to the Soviet BRDM-1, and was visually similar. There were differences, however: the Hungarian vehicle's engine was at the rear, and it had two water jets for swimming instead of one. It entered service with the Hungarian army in 1964, and two years later entered service with the Czech and Polish armies. In Czech service it was known as the OT-65.

The hull was of welded-steel armour. The driver sat at the front left, with the commander to his right. Behind them was a troop compartment that could hold four soldiers. The only means of entry or exit was a roof hatch, which opened to either side. The hatch covers could be fixed vertically, providing some measure of protection when using the 7.62mm SGMB machine gun. Six firing ports were fitted: two on each side, and two in the rear.

The engine compartment was to the rear of the troop compartment. Like the BRDM-1, the FÚG had four small wheels that were normally retracted into the hull, but could be lowered by the driver to improve cross-country performance. The FÚG was fully amphibious. Before entering the water, a trim vane, normally kept under the nose, was erected and the bilge pumps switched on. In the water, the vehicle was propelled by a pair of water jets.

Standard equipment included infra-red driving lights, and some models had an infra-red searchlight and central tyre pressure regulation system. There was no NBC protection for the crew. Armament was a single pintle-mounted 7.62mm SGMB machine gun, operated by a crew member with the roof hatches open.

An NBC reconnaissance version, the D-442VS or FÚG-US, was used to mark contaminated areas. It had racks containing marker poles with pennants, to be fired into the ground.

The OT-65A was a Czech modification, fitted with the same manually-operated turret as the OT-62B armoured personnel carrier. This had a 7.62mm M59T machine gun, and an 82mm T-21 recoilless gun mounted externally on the right side. An infra-red searchlight was mounted to the right of the recoilless gun. The T-21 could be aimed and fired from inside the turret, but could only be reloaded from outside. It had a maximum range of 2,500m, although the effective range was significantly less, at 300m to 450m. The 82mm HEAT projectile could penetrate up to 230mm of armour.

Specifications: FÚG/OT-65 (OT-65A in brackets)

Crew: 2 + 4 dismounts
Combat weight: 7,000kg
Length: 5.79m
Width: 2.5m
Height: 1.91m (2.25m)
Ground clearance: 0.34m

Maximum road speed: 87km/hour
Maximum road range: 600km
Gradient: 60%
Vertical obstacle: 0.4m
Trench: 1.2m
Armour (max): 13mm

ARMAMENT (FÚG):
1x 7.62mm SGMB machine gun (1,250 rounds)

ARMAMENT (OT-65A):
1x 7.62mm M59T machine gun
1x 82mm T-21 recoilless gun

Self-Propelled Anti-Aircraft Weapons

Soviet army air defence was based on the principles of mass, mix, mobility, and integration. Sheer numbers provided mass; the variety of complementary weapon systems provided mix. The design of the systems emphasised mobility, and the weapons were integrated at every level, from platoon to front.

In 1944, the Soviet army trialled a 37mm V-47 AA gun mounted on an SU-76 chassis, designated ZSU-37. In 1945, they experimented with a naval twin 25mm gun on a similar vehicle, designated ZSU-25. These vehicles were produced in small numbers for trials, but neither was adopted for service. Both designs suffered from slow turret traverse, making them ineffective against low-flying aircraft.

BTR-40A & BTR-152A

These were modified BTR-40 and BTR-152 APCs which entered service in 1952. Each had a pair of 14.5mm KPV machine guns mounted over the troop compartment in a simple, manually operated turret. The turret had 360° traverse, 80° elevation, and 5° depression, but minimal armoured protection for the gunner. In addition to AA support, the BTR-40A and BTR-152A were used to provide general fire support against ground targets. The guns had an effective range of around 2,000m against ground targets, and 1,400m against airborne targets. The slow traverse speed of the turret and the ineffectiveness of the simple sights severely limited their usefulness as AA vehicles.

Further AA variants of the BTR-152 were developed. The BTR-152D had four 14.5mm KPV machine guns, and the BTR-152E, introduced in 1955, had the same twin KPV mount as the BTR-152A, but was based on the BTR-152V chassis.

SPECIFICATIONS: BTR-40A

Crew: 5 passengers
Combat weight: 5,300kg
Length: 5m
Width: 1.9m
Height: 2.5m
Ground clearance: 0.3m
Maximum road speed: 80km/hour
Maximum road range: 285km
Gradient: 60%
Vertical obstacle: 0.47m
Trench: 0.7m
Armament: 2x 14.5mm KPV machine gun (2,400 rounds)
Armour: 6-8mm

SPECIFICATIONS: BTR-152A

Crew: 4
Combat weight: 9,600kg
Length: 6.83m
Width: 2.32m
Height: 2.05m

Ground clearance: 0.3m
Maximum road speed: 65km/hour
Maximum road range: 780km
Gradient: 55%
Vertical obstacle: 0.6m
Trench: 0.69m
Armament: 2x 14.5mm KPV machine gun (2,000 rounds)

Armour:
Front: 13.5mm @ 35° [Effective: 16mm]
Side: 9mm @ 7° [Effective: 9mm]
Rear: 9mm
Belly: 4mm

ZSU-57-2

The ZSU-57-2 entered service in 1955. The hull was based on a lightened T-54 chassis, with much lighter armour and four road wheels rather the T-54's five. Two air-cooled 57mm S-68 guns were fitted in a large, boxy, open-topped turret. A tarpaulin cover was carried for protection against inclement weather.

The guns had optical sights (initially with no rangefinder, though a rangefinder was later added) and the turret had powered traverse and elevation. The sights were configured to allow use in a secondary role as a ground support vehicle. The guns had a maximum effective range of around 4,000m. The powered turret was a significant improvement over earlier vehicles, but the lack of radar limited the ZSU-57-2 to use in clear weather. It did not have NBC protection or amphibious capability.

ZSU-57-2

Specifications: ZSU-57-2

Crew: 6
Combat weight: 28.1 tonnes
Length: 6.22m
Width: 3.27m
Height: 2.75m
Maximum road speed: 50km/hour
Maximum road range: 420km
Gradient: 60%
Vertical obstacle: 0.8m
Trench: 2.7m
Armament: 2x 57mm S-68 guns (300 rounds)
Armour: 8-15mm

ZSU-23-4 Shilka

The ZSU-23-4 entered service in 1966, as a replacement for the much less effective ZSU-57-2. The chassis was based on a

ZSU-23-4 Shilka

modified ASU-85, and it had an enclosed turret holding four water-cooled 2A7 23mm guns (the gun mounting was designated AZP-23). Although the choice of a 23mm gun reduced the effective range, it had a much higher rate of fire, leading to a greater probability of a hit. The vehicle had NBC protection and infra-red night-vision equipment, but no amphibious capability.

The ZSU-23-4 had a Gun Dish radar for acquisition and tracking, connected to an analogue computer, allowing operation in all weather conditions. The radar could acquire targets at a range of up to 20km, and track targets at up to 18km. Optical sights were fitted for use as a backup and in heavy ECM environments.

The large number of electronic vacuum tubes in the fire-control computer generated a great deal of heat, which caused problems with cooling. In 1966, the ZSU-23-4V entered service, which had changes to the venting covers and removed the heat exchanger from the turret roof. In 1970, the ZSU-23-4V1 was introduced. This had an improved computer, and ventilation system cases at the front of the turret. The ZSU-23-4M, introduced in 1973, had further cooling improvements and enhanced ECCM. From 1977, vehicles were fitted with an improved IFF system and designated ZSU-23-4MZ. This IFF system was retrofitted to existing ZSU-23-4M systems.

Specifications: ZSU-23-4 Shilka

Crew: 4
Combat weight: 19 tonnes
Length: 6.54m
Width: 3.13m
Height: 3.75m (2.6m with radar down)
Ground clearance: 0.35m
Maximum road speed: 50km/hour
Maximum road range: 450km
Gradient: 60%
Vertical obstacle: 1m
Trench: 2.4m
Armament: 4x 23mm 2A7 guns (2,000 rounds)

Armour:
Hull: 15mm max
Turret: 9.4mm

2S6

The 2S6 entered limited service in 1982. Its layout was similar to the ZSU-23-4, with a large turret mounted in the centre of the hull and the engine at the rear. The 2S6 was armed with a pair of 2A38 30mm cannons (one on each side of the turret), and four SA-19 Grison missiles (two on each side of the turret). A target acquisition radar was fitted at the rear of the turret, and a

2S6M

tracking radar at the front. The guns were stabilised in both planes to allow firing on the move, but the missiles could only be fired when stationary. The vehicle was armoured to a level sufficient to provide protection from small arms and shell splinters.

In 1986, the main production system, the 2S6M, entered service. This increased the missile load from four to eight missiles (four on each side of the turret). The fire-control programmes were improved, and improved guns (2A38M) and missiles (Soviet designation 9M311M) were fitted.

Specifications: 2S6M

Crew: 4
Combat weight: 34 tonnes
Length: 7.93m
Width: 3.24m
Height: 4.01m (3.36m with radar stowed)

Maximum road speed: 65km/hour
Maximum road range: 500km
Vertical obstacle: 1m
Trench: 2m

ARMAMENT:
8x SA-19 Grison missiles (2S6: 4x SA-19 Grison missiles)
2x 30mm 2A38M cannon (1,904 rounds) (2S6: 2x 30mm 2A38 cannon)

SA-4 GANEF

The SA-4 Ganef (Krug) was the first self-propelled surface-to-air missile system deployed by the Soviet Union. It was built on a new tracked chassis, later used as the basis for the 2S3 self-propelled howitzer. The launch vehicle carried two missiles on an elevating turntable, but had no on-board fire control. The vehicle had NBC protection and infra-red driving lights, but was not amphibious.

The missile had a maximum range of 55km, a maximum altitude of 27.4km, and a 135kg HE warhead with terminal semi-active radar homing. Initial guidance came from the radar vehicle via radio link, although an optical backup could be used if required. A later version of the missile had a shorter minimum range but improved performance at low altitudes. Each battery usually had both versions of the missile, since they had complementary strengths and weaknesses.

The first version of the system entered service in 1965, with a modified version (Krug-A) entering full-scale production and service in 1967. Each battery had a Pat Hand radar, mounted on the same vehicle as the launch vehicle, for fire control and guidance. Spare missiles were carried on TZM transloader vehicles, based on Ural 375 lorries, with on-board cranes for

SA-4 Ganef

transferring missiles. Reloading the TEL vehicle took 10 to 15 minutes.

SPECIFICATIONS: SA-4 GANEF

Crew: 3-5
Combat weight: 28.2 tonnes
Length: 7.5m (9.46m including missiles)
Width: 3.2m
Height: 4.47m (including missiles)
Ground clearance: 0.44m
Maximum road speed: 35km/hour
Maximum road range: 780km
Gradient: 60%
Vertical obstacle: 1m
Armour: 15mm max

Number of missiles: 2
Missile diameter: 860mm
Warhead weight: 135kg
Missile length: SA-4A: 8.8m, SA-4B: 8.4m
Missile weight: 2,453kg
Missile range: SA-4A: 55km, SA-4B: 50km
Reload time: 10-15 minutes

SA-6 Gainful

After various difficulties in development, the SA-6 Gainful was accepted for service in 1967. It was the first Soviet SAM system designed to engage low-flying aircraft, and made extensive use of transistors and printed circuit boards instead of vacuum tubes. The launch and radar vehicles had hulls based on a modified ASU-85 chassis, similar to that used for the ZSU-23-4. Like the ZSU-23-4, the vehicles had infra-red night-vision equipment, NBC protection, and no amphibious capability.

The missile was unconventional in design, using an integral solid rocket engine that fell away once its fuel was expended, leaving a solid fuel ramjet to take over. This design offered a high maximum speed of Mach 2.5 and was very simple, with low unit and maintenance costs, although performance suffered at high altitudes.

The launch vehicle carried three missiles on an elevating launcher with 360° traverse. The radar vehicle carried a Straight Flush radar. Each battery had four launch vehicles and one radar vehicle. The battery was controlled from the radar vehicle, which was connected to the launch vehicles by cable or radio link.

SA-6 Gainful

Specifications: SA-6 Gainful

Crew: 3
Combat weight: 14 tonnes
Length: 6.8m

Width: 3.2m
Height: 3.45m
Ground clearance: 0.35m
Maximum road speed: 45km/hour
Maximum road range: 250km
Gradient: 60%
Vertical obstacle: 1m
Trench: 2.4m
Armour: 9mm max
Number of missiles: 3
Missile diameter: 335mm
Warhead weight: 59kg
Missile length: 5.8m
Missile weight: 599kg
Missile range: 24km
Reload time: 10 minutes

SA-8 Gecko

The SA-8 Gecko entered service in 1970, and was notable for being the first Soviet surface-to-air missile system to be fully self-contained, with the tracking radars mounted on the same vehicle as the missiles. The TELAR was based on an unarmoured BAZ-5937 chassis, and was amphibious and air-transportable. The missiles and radar were housed on a rotating mount at the centre of the vehicle. The Land Roll radar was in the centre of the mount, with a small antenna on each side. These small antennae were used to guide the missiles, allowing the vehicle to control two missiles simultaneously. A low-light television system was mounted above the Land Roll radar, and could be used to guide the missiles in a heavy ECM environment. Two missiles were mounted on rails on either side of the radar.

SA-8b Gecko Mod-0

In 1975, the SA-8b Gecko Mod-0 was introduced. This version was easily distinguished from the initial version, since it carried six missiles instead of four, housed in sealed containers. In 1980, another new version (SA-8b Gecko Mod-1) added an IFF antenna and improved missiles, with increased range and maximum height.

A dedicated reload vehicle was developed on the same chassis, and carried 18 missiles in a cargo compartment covered by a tarpaulin. A crane was fitted to facilitate reloading, which took around five minutes. An SA-8 battery had four TELAR vehicles and two reload vehicles.

Specifications: SA-8b Gecko Mod-0

Crew: 5
Combat weight: 17.5 tonnes
Length: 9.14m
Width: 2.8m

Height: 4.2m
Ground clearance: 0.4m
Maximum road speed: 80km/hour
Maximum road range: 500km
Number of missiles: 6
Missile diameter: 210mm
Warhead weight: 20kg
Missile length: 3.16m
Missile weight: 126kg
Missile range: 10km
Reload time: 10 minutes

SA-9 Gaskin

The SA-9 Gaskin entered service in 1968, and was based on a BRDM-2 chassis with the retractable belly wheels removed. The turret was replaced with a mounting for four 9M31M Strela-1 missiles. The missiles were normally folded down flat to the hull roof for transport, then raised for firing. An improved missile (SA-9B Gaskin Mod-0) was introduced in 1970.

The vehicle was amphibious, using the same water-jet propulsion system as the BRDM-2, and had NBC protection. There was a crew of three: driver, gunner, and commander. The driver and commander were supplied with periscopes and infra-red night-vision equipment.

Each SA-9 battery normally had a single SA-9 Mod-A vehicle, mounting a Flat Box A passive radar detection system in addition to the missiles. It should be noted that this was a passive system, which simply detected radar emissions from approaching aircraft to provide a bearing. The gunner would traverse the launch mounting to the appropriate bearing, then acquire the target visually.

The SA-9 was normally deployed in tandem with the ZSU-23-4 anti-aircraft gun, so that the two systems complemented one another. Missiles were fired in pairs to increase the chance of a hit, and used infra-red, heat-seeking sensors to home in on their target. The SA-9 vehicle itself did not normally carry reload missiles. In foreign service, however, they were sometimes seen with a missile attached to each side of the hull.

Specifications: SA-9 Gaskin

Crew: 4
Combat weight: 7,000kg
Length: 5.75m
Width: 2.35m
Height: 2.31m
Ground clearance: 0.43m
Maximum road speed: 100km/hour
Maximum road range: 750km
Gradient: 60%
Vertical obstacle: 0.4m
Trench: 1.25m
Number of missiles: 4
Missile diameter: 120mm
Warhead weight: 2.6kg
Missile length: 1.8m
Missile weight: 32kg
Missile range: 6.5km (Mod-0: 8km)
Reload time: 5 minutes

Armour:
Hull front upper: 5mm @ 80° [Effective: 29mm]
Hull front lower: 7mm @ 45° [Effective: 10mm]
Hull nose plate: 14mm @ 14° [Effective: 14mm]

Hull sides upper: 7mm @ 18° [Effective: 7.1mm]
Hull sides lower: 7mm
Hull rear: 7mm
Hull top: 7mm
Belly: 2-3mm

SA-10 Grumble

After a protracted development period, the SA-10A Grumble became operational in 1980. The initial version was designed for deployment at fixed sites. The launcher was a trailer, towed by a KrAZ-260V 6x6 tractor unit and positioned on concrete pads for firing, stabilised by four hydraulic jacks.

A mobile system, designated SA-10B Grumble Mod-1 by NATO, was deployed in 1985. It was based on a MAZ-7910 8x8 chassis, with four missiles, engagement radar, and a fire-control system. The missiles were stored in cylinders, which were kept horizontal during transit. Before firing, four hydraulic jacks were lowered and the missiles were raised to 90°. Time needed to prepare for firing was around five minutes. There were two variants of the TEL: the 5P85S had control logic and datalink hardware, while the 5P85D had no control hardware, and was controlled by a 5P85S. A typical battery would consist of one 5P85S TEL, two 5P85D TELs, and one 5N63S mobile Flap Lid B radar.

Two versions of the missile were developed. The first (5V55K) entered service in 1980, then the improved 5V55R entered service in 1984. The 5V55K used command guidance and had a maximum range of 47km. The 5V55R used semi-automatic radar homing, had almost double the range (90km), and an increased warhead size.

SA-10 Grumble battery

Specifications: SA-10 Grumble

Length: 12.1m
Width: 3.05m
Maximum road speed: 60km/hour
Range: 850km
Number of missiles: 4
Missile diameter: 450mm
Warhead weight: 5V55K: 100kg, 5V55R: 133kg
Missile length: 7m
Missile weight: 5V55K: 1,450kg, 5V55R: 1,664kg
Missile range: 5V55K: 47km, 5V55R: 90km

SA-11 Gadfly

Development of a system to replace the SA-6, which was to become the 9K37 Buk (known to NATO as the SA-11 Gadfly),

SA-11 Gadfly

began in the early 1970s, and was accepted for service in 1980. An SA-11 battery consisted of two launch vehicles and one reload vehicle. The target acquisition radar was at battalion level, but each launch vehicle had an on-board fire control radar. It took a battery around five minutes to prepare for action after moving, and five minutes to prepare for movement.

The launch vehicle was based on a tracked chassis and had NBC protection. A traversing mount was fitted on the hull, with a Fire Dome radar at the front and an elevating launcher for four missiles at the rear. The reload vehicle was similar, but had a crane in place of the radar. The reload vehicle could launch missiles, but would have to rely on a nearby launch vehicle's radar for guidance. The missiles had a maximum speed of Mach 3, a maximum range of 30km, and a maximum height of 14km. Semi-active radar homing guidance was used, although an electro-optical guidance system could be used in heavy ECM environments, with commands sent to the missile via a radio link.

An improved version of the SA-11, the 9K37M1 Buk-M1 was accepted for service in 1983. This had improved radar performance, kill probability, and ECM resistance. A new threat-classification system was fitted, which analysed radar return signals to classify targets without IFF.

SPECIFICATIONS: SA-11 GADFLY

Ground clearance: 0.45m
Maximum road speed: 65km/hour
Maximum road range: 500km
Number of missiles: 4
Missile diameter: 400mm
Warhead weight: 70kg
Missile length: 5.55m
Missile weight: 690kg
Missile range: 30km

SA-12 GLADIATOR

The SA-12 Gladiator replaced the SA-4 Ganef, and was designed to provide protection against cruise missiles as well as aircraft. The missile had the same design roots as the SA-10 Grumble, but was mounted on a tracked TELAR based on the MT-T chassis, with four missiles and a guidance radar. A separate Grill Pan radar was used for tracking. The reload vehicle was very similar to the TELAR vehicle, but had a crane instead of a radar. It could launch missiles, but needed a TELAR vehicle to control them.

SPECIFICATIONS: SA-12 GLADIATOR

Length: 8.71m
Width: 3.28m

SA-12 Gladiator

Maximum road speed: 65km/hour
Maximum road range: 500km
Gradient: 60%
Vertical obstacle: 0.65m
Trench: 2.5m
Number of missiles: 4
Warhead weight: 150kg
Missile weight: 420kg
Missile range: 75km

SA-13 Gopher

After some problems in development, the SA-13 Gopher was approved for service in 1976. The SA-13 was based on an MT-LB, but without the machine gun turret. A launcher fitted over the cargo compartment carried four 9K35 Strela-10 missiles and was folded down flat to the roof when in transit. A parabolic antenna was fixed in the centre of the missiles, for the range-only

SA-13 Gopher

Hat Box radar. This radar was used to ensure that a target was within range before launching missiles. A Flat Box B passive radar detection system was fitted to most vehicles, but not to the battery commander's vehicle. Eight reload missiles were carried within the vehicle.

The Strela-10 infra-red, heat-seeking missile offered several improvements over the SA-9's Strela-1. It had an improved, cooled seeker head, which could home in on an aircraft from any angle, not only onto the jet exhaust. The SA-13 launcher could fire the older Strela-1 missile as well as the Strela-10. The Strela-10 travelled at just under Mach 2 to a maximum range of 5km and maximum height of 3.5km. In 1981 an improved missile was introduced, which had a heavier warhead and improved ECCM, proximity fuse, and engine.

The SA-13 had NBC protection and was fully amphibious, propelled in the water by its tracks.

Specifications: SA-13 Gopher

Crew: 2 + 11 passengers
Combat weight: 11,900kg
Maximum payload: 2,000kg
Maximum towed load: 6,500kg
Length: 6.45m
Width: 2.86m
Height: 1.87m
Ground clearance: 0.4m
Maximum road speed: 62km/hour
Maximum road range: 500km
Gradient: 60%
Vertical obstacle: 0.6m
Trench: 2.41m
Armour: 4-10mm
Armament: 4x 9K35 Strela-10 missiles (plus eight reloads)
Number of missiles: 4
Missile diameter: 123mm
Warhead weight: 5kg
Missile length: 2.2m
Missile weight: 41kg
Missile range: 5km
Reload time: 3 minutes

BTR-ZD

The BTR-ZD was a standard BTR-D airborne APC. However, the BTR-ZD carried two surface-to-air missile teams equipped with SA-7, SA-14, or SA-16. It also had a ZU-23-2 twin 23mm AA gun, which could be towed behind the vehicle or mounted on top of the troop compartment. Ramps were carried to assist with loading and unloading the guns onto the vehicle. The ZU-23-2

BTR-ZD

had simple optical sights, and full 360° traverse, whether mounted on the vehicle or used separately. Like the BTR-D, the BTR-ZD had NBC protection and amphibious capability.

Specifications: BTR-ZD

Combat weight: 8,000kg
Length: 5.89m
Width: 2.63m
Height: 1.67m
Ground clearance: 0.1-0.45m
Maximum road speed: 60km/hour
Maximum road range: 500km

Armament:
1x ZU-23-2 AA gun
2x SAM launchers (SA-7, SA-14 or SA-16)

Armour:
Hull front upper: 15mm @ 78° [Effective: 72mm]
Hull front lower: 15mm @ 50° [Effective: 23mm]
Hull side: 10mm
Hull rear: 10mm

M53/59 (Czechoslovakia)

When the Czech army was looking for an APC in the mid-1950s, Praga put forward an armoured version of its V3S 6x6 lorry. The design lost out to a Tatra design based on the German Second World War Sdkfz 251, but it was used as the basis for a self-propelled anti-aircraft gun. Entering service in the late 1950s, it mounted a modified version of the M53 twin 30mm anti-aircraft gun at the rear. The guns could, and often were, dismounted for use on the ground.

The vehicle had a welded hull with the engine at the front, crew compartment in the centre, and armament at the rear. The driver sat on the left, with the commander to his right. They had a windscreen to their front, which was fitted with an armoured cover with a vision slit. Each had a side door with vision slit, and the top section of the doors could be folded down. The commander also had a clear dome on the roof to for full 360° observation. The loaders were seated behind the driver and commander, facing backward, each with a vision slit to the side. A two-piece hatch cover at the rear folded down, forming a platform for the loaders when in action.

The two 30mm cannons had full 360° traverse, could be elevated to 85°, and depressed to -10°. The crew compartment limited depression over the frontal arc to +2°, and a steel plate prevented the guns hitting the commander's dome. Elevation, depression, and traverse were all hydraulic, and manual controls

M53/59

were provided as a backup. The gunner was seated to the left of the guns with armour protection to the front, side, and rear, although the position was open topped. Originally the barrels had multi-baffle muzzle brakes, but these were later replaced by conical flash hiders. Barrels could be quickly changed, with spares kept at regimental level.

The cannons were fully automatic, with a cyclic rate of fire of 450-500 rounds per minute each, and a practical rate of fire of 150 rounds per minute each. Note that the towed version of the guns had a lower rate of fire, because they did not have magazines, whereas the M53-59 guns were fed from 50-round vertical magazines. Maximum horizontal range was 9,700m, maximum vertical range was 6,300m, and effective anti-aircraft range was around 3,000m.

API and HEI projectiles were available. Three magazines were carried on either side of the gun platform, with more fastened to the floor in the rear of the crew compartment. The vehicle was limited to use in clear weather, had no NBC protection, night-vision equipment, amphibious capability, or central tyre pressure regulation system.

SPECIFICATIONS: M53/59

Crew: 5
Combat weight: 10.3 tonnes
Length: 6.92m
Width: 2.35m
Height: 2.95m (2.56m without magazines)
Maximum road speed: 60km/hour
Maximum road range: 500km
Gradient: 60%
Vertical obstacle: 0.46m
Trench: 0.69m
Armament: 2x 30mm M53 guns (800 rounds)
Armour: 10mm max

Self-Propelled Guns, Howitzers, and Mortars

The Soviet army, and the Russian army before it, referred to artillery as the "god of war", and was deservedly proud of the artillery arm. During the Second World War, little interest was shown in self-propelled artillery, with only multiple rocket launchers (commonly referred to by the nickname "Katyusha") being developed as mobile systems. The only self-propelled guns were tank destroyers and assault guns designed for direct fire, rather than artillery guns and howitzers intended to provide indirect fire. Development of self-propelled guns, howitzers, and mortars started in the late 1960s, probably helped by the removal from power of Khrushchev, a firm proponent of missiles and rockets.

SU-76

In 1942, the Soviet army had an urgent need for a tank destroyer, and the SU-76 was hastily developed to meet that requirement. First used in combat in early 1943, it was found to be inadequate for the anti-tank role, and so was repurposed to infantry support. Over 12,000 vehicles were built, but production stopped in 1945.

The chassis was a longer and wider version of that used on the T-70 light tank, armed with a modified version of the ZIS-3 76mm divisional gun. Originally, it had engines on either side of the hull and a fully-armoured fighting compartment. This was not a success and only a few were built. The design was changed to have engines mounted in tandem and a partially-armoured fighting compartment, creating the SU-76M.

The hull was of all-welded construction. The driver sat at the front centre, with a single-piece hatch cover and a periscope. The engines were mounted in tandem on the right side of the hull, toward the rear, with the fuel tank to the left of the driver.

The open-topped fighting compartment was at the rear of the vehicle. A tubular frame allowed a tarpaulin cover to be fitted to give protection against inclement weather. Access was via a single door in the rear, and firing ports were fitted on either side of the fighting compartment. The commander had a vision port to the right of the armament, with the gunner's sight to the left of the gun.

The 76mm gun was mounted to the left of centre, and had a double-baffle muzzle brake. Elevation and traverse were both manual, and it fired the same types of ammunition as the PT-76 light tank. 60 rounds of ammunition were carried, and during the Second World War many vehicles carried a 7.62mm machine gun for use against aircraft.

The SU-76 did not have NBC protection, night-vision equipment, or an amphibious capability.

Specifications: SU-76M

Crew: 4
Combat weight: 11.2 tonnes
Length: 5.0m
Width: 2.74m

SU-76M

Height: 2.1m
Ground clearance: 0.3m
Maximum road speed: 45km/hour
Maximum road range: 360km
Gradient: 47%
Vertical obstacle: 0.65m
Armament: 1x 76.2mm gun (60 rounds)

ARMOUR:
Hull glacis: 25mm @ 30° [Effective: 29mm]
Hull nose: 35mm @ 60° [Effective: 70mm]
Superstructure front: 25 @ 27° [Effective: 28mm]
Superstructure side: 12mm @ 17° [Effective: 13mm]
Mantlet: 14mm
Lower hull side: 16mm
Hull rear: 15mm
Belly: 10mm

ISU-122

Like the heavier ISU-152, the ISU-122 was based on the IS-2 tank chassis. The armament was mounted in an armoured superstructure at the front, with the engine and transmission at the rear. The main armament, an 122mm A-19S gun, was mounted to the right of centre, with the driver seated to the left. Elevation and traverse were both manual. A 12.7mm DShKM machine gun was mounted on the roof for anti-aircraft use. Long-range fuel tanks were fitted on the sides of the hull, at the rear.

The A-19S was a development of the towed A-19 gun, and had a rate of fire of three rounds per minute. HE-FRAG, concrete piercing, and AP-T rounds were available. The range of the HE-FRAG round was reduced by the gun's elevation to 13,400m.

In 1944, the original ISU-122 was replaced in production by the ISU-122S. This was armed with a 122mm D-25S gun, a development of the D-25 used in the IS-2, IS-3, and IS-4 heavy tanks. An improved breech compared to the A-19S meant that the rate of fire was increased to six rounds per minute. An MSh-17 gun sight was fitted for direct fire. Unlike the ISU-122, the ISU-122S had a double-baffle muzzle brake.

Specifications: ISU-122S

Crew: 5
Combat weight: 46.5 tonnes
Length: 6.8m (10.1m including gun)
Width: 3.07m
Height: 2.47m
Ground clearance: 0.46m
Maximum road speed: 37km/hour

ISU-122

Maximum road range: 150km (306km with long-range fuel tanks)
Gradient: 60%
Vertical obstacle: 1m

ARMAMENT:
1x 122mm D-25S (30 rounds)
1x 12.7mm DShKM MG (250 rounds)

ARMOUR:
Hull glacis: 110mm @ 70° [Effective: 322mm]
Mantlet: 90mm
Upper hull sides: 90mm
Hull top: 25mm
Hull rear: 22-64mm
Belly: 19mm

ISU-152

Almost identical to the earlier SU-152, the ISU-152 was based on an IS-2 chassis, whereas the SU-152 was based on the KV-2. The 152mm ML-20S gun, a development of the ML-20, was mounted in an armoured superstructure at the front of the vehicle, to the right of centre. The gun was shorter than the one fitted on the ISU-122, and had a multi-baffle muzzle brake.

The driver was seated to the left of the main armament. Hand rails were fitted on the outside of the vehicle to allow infantry to be carried into action, and a 12.7mm DShKM machine gun was mounted on the roof for anti-aircraft use. The very limited on-board ammunition store of only twenty rounds meant that frequent resupply was required. Elevation and traverse were both manual, and the maximum elevation of the gun limited the range of the HE-FRAG round to 9,000m. Long-range fuel tanks were fitted on the sides of the hull, at the rear.

SPECIFICATIONS: ISU-152

Crew: 5
Combat weight: 46.5 tonnes
Length: 6.8m (9.05m including gun)
Width: 3.07m
Height: 2.47m
Ground clearance: 0.46m
Maximum road speed: 37km/hour
Maximum road range: 150km (306km with long-range fuel tanks)
Gradient: 60%
Vertical obstacle: 1m

ISU-152

ARMAMENT:
1x 152mm ML-20S (20 rounds)
1x 12.7mm DShKM MG (250 rounds)

ARMOUR:
Hull glacis: 110mm @ 70° [Effective: 322mm]
Mantlet: 90mm
Upper hull sides: 90mm
Hull top: 25mm
Hull rear: 22-64mm
Belly: 19mm

2S1 GVOZDIKA

The first prototype 2S1 vehicles were built in 1969. It was accepted for service in 1970 and began volume production in 1971. The hull was made of welded steel, based on the automotive components and running gear of the MT-LB. The driver sat at the front with the engine behind him, and the turret and fighting compartment at the rear. Within the turret, the commander sat on the left, with the gunner below and in front of him, and the loader to the right. The gun had sights for indirect and direct fire.

The main armament was a 2A31 122mm howitzer, based on the D-30 towed howitzer. It had a fume extractor and double-baffle muzzle brake, and a remote-controlled lock on the hull to fix the barrel in place during transit. A rate of fire of 5-8 rounds per minute could be maintained for a protracted period. 40 rounds of ammunition were carried in the vehicle, the usual load being 32 HE, six smoke, and two HEAT-FS. Standard practice during a fire mission was for ammunition to be supplied from outside the vehicle. When firing HE, the gun had a maximum range of 15.3km. The HEAT-FS warhead could penetrate around 460mm of standard steel armour. Chemical and HE-RAP ammunition was also available, the latter extending the maximum range to 21.9km.

The 2S1's suspension could be adjusted to make the vehicle shorter, a useful feature when transporting by air. The standard tracks were 400mm wide, but like the MT-LB, 670mm wide tracks could be fitted for use in snow, swampy ground, etc. The 2S1 had NBC protection, infra-red driving lights, and a small infra-red searchlight on the commander's cupola. It was fully amphibious, propelled in the water by its tracks. Before entering the water, a bilge pump was switched on, shrouds were fitted to the hull front, water deflectors were lowered at the rear, the trim vane was erected at the front of the hull, and covers were fitted around the engine air intakes. Only 30 rounds could be carried when swimming; any excess had to be removed before entering the water.

SPECIFICATIONS: 2S1 GVOZDIKA

Crew: 4 + 2 in ammunition carrier
Combat weight: 15.7 tonnes

2S1 Gvozdika

Length: 7.26m
Width: 2.85m
Height: 2.287m
Ground clearance: 0.4m
Maximum road speed: 61.5km/hour
Maximum road range: 500km
Gradient: 77%
Vertical obstacle: 0.7m
Armament: 1x 122mm 2A31 howitzer (40 rounds)

ARMOUR:
Hull: 15mm
Turret: 10-20mm

2S3 AKATSIYA

Production of the 2S3 started in 1970, although it was not accepted for service until late 1971. The hull was based on an improved version of the SA-4 Ganef chassis, with a more powerful 520hp engine, upgraded track and suspension. The hull was welded steel, with the driver in the front to the left, the engine to his right, and the turret at the rear. The commander was seated in the left of the turret, the gunner forward and below him, and the loader on the right. The gun had sights for direct fire as well as indirect fire.

Main armament was a 2A33 152mm howitzer. Almost identical to the D-20 towed howitzer, it was fitted with a fume extractor and travelling lock, which was remotely operated by the driver from his seat. Traverse and elevation were powered, though manual controls were also provided. 33 rounds of ammunition were carried in the rear of the hull. Normally, ammunition was supplied from outside the vehicle and passed in through hatches in the rear, the internal ammunition being reserved for immediate use. HE-FRAG ammunition was most commonly used, though HEAT-FS, HE-RAP, AP-T, illuminating, smoke, incendiary, flechette, and scatter mine ammunition were also available. Maximum range was 18.5km with conventional ammunition, 24km when firing HE-RAP.

A 7.62mm PKT machine gun was mounted on the commander's cupola. This could be aimed and fired by remote control from inside the turret. The 2S3 had NBC protection, infra-red driving lights, a small white light/infra-red searchlight mounted forward of the commander's hatch, and a self-entrenching blade at the front of the hull. It did not have an amphibious capability.

The 2S3M, introduced in 1975, increased the on-board ammunition load to 46 rounds, 12 of which were in a rotating carousel to facilitate faster loading. The 2S3M1, introduced in 1987, added a data terminal connected to the battery commander's vehicle, allowing fire commands to be instantly

2S3 Akatsiya

displayed in the fire vehicles. It also had an improved sight and new laser-guided, rocket-assisted projectiles were available.

SPECIFICATIONS: 2S3 AKATSIYA

Crew: 4 + 2 in ammunition carrier
Combat weight: 27.5 tonnes
Length: 7.7m (8.4m including gun)
Width: 3.25m
Height: 3.05m
Ground clearance: 0.45m
Maximum road speed: 60km/hour
Maximum road range: 500km
Gradient: 60%
Vertical obstacle: 0.7m
Trench: 3m

Armament:
1x 152mm 2A33 howitzer (33 rounds, 2S3M/M1: 46 rounds)
1x 7.62mm PKT MG (1,500 rounds)

Armour:
Hull: 15mm max
Turret: 20mm max

2S4 Tyulpan

Introduced in 1970, the 2S4 mounted a 240mm breech-loading mortar on a tracked vehicle based on the GMZ minelayer chassis. The mortar, complete with baseplate, lay along the length of the vehicle when in transit. To deploy, the mortar was rotated around a hinge at the rear of the vehicle, so that it came to rest facing away from the vehicle to the rear, with the baseplate on the ground. Elevation was from +45° to +80°, with 8° of traverse.

Four men were carried in the vehicle, though a total of nine were required to load and fire the mortar. Twelve mortar bombs were carried in the vehicle, and a small hand-operated crane was fitted to the rear to facilitate loading. The mortar had a rate of fire of one round per minute, and could fire HE, chemical, and nuclear rounds. The 240mm mortar was the first Soviet artillery piece to be equipped with nuclear ammunition.

The vehicle hull had welded steel armour, with the driver at the front left and the engine to his right. To the rear of the driver was the commander, who was provided with a raised cupola, on which was mounted a 7.62mm PKT machine gun. The vehicle provided NBC protection for the crew while they were inside, though they had to exit the vehicle to operate the mortar.

2S4 Tyulpan

Specifications: 2S4 Tyulpan

Crew: 4 + 5 in ammunition carrier
Combat weight: 30 tonnes
Length: 8.5m
Width: 3.2m
Height: 3.2m
Ground clearance: 0.46m
Maximum road speed: 50km/hour
Maximum road range: 500km
Gradient: 65%
Vertical obstacle: 1.1m
Armour: 15-20mm

Armament:
1x 240mm mortar (12 rounds)
1x 7.62mm PKT MG

2S5 GIATSINT-S

In 1968, development began on a new 152mm gun, which was intended to be used in both towed and self-propelled versions. Production of both towed (2A36) and self-propelled (2S5) guns began in 1976. The 2S5 had a welded steel hull, and a self-entrenching blade was mounted on the front. The engine was at the front right of the vehicle, and could use diesel or aviation fuel. The vehicle provided NBC protection when sealed, though the gun could not be operated from inside the vehicle.

The driver sat to the left of the engine, and was provided with day and passive night periscopes. The vehicle commander sat behind the driver in a slightly raised superstructure with a cupola, on which was mounted a 7.62mm PKT machine gun and a white light/IR searchlight. The machine gun could be operated from within the vehicle. The three remaining crew members were seated in a compartment at the rear of the vehicle, entering via a ramp at the rear. They were provided with periscopes, but these periscopes did not have any night-vision capability.

The 2A37 152mm gun was mounted on the vehicle roof in an open mount at the rear, and had a multi-baffled muzzle brake. Sights for direct and indirect fire were included, and a travelling lock was used when in transit. A large spade was deployed at the rear of the vehicle before firing, to provide extra stability.

The gunlayer sat to the left of the gun, and had a simple shield to his front. 30 projectiles and charges were carried in the rear of the vehicle. The projectiles were in a carousel and the charges were in three rows of ten on a conveyor belt. Maximum rate of fire was five to six rounds per minute.

2S5 Giatsint-S in firing position

SPECIFICATIONS: 2S5 GIATSINT-S

Crew: 5
Combat weight: 28.2 tonnes
Length: 8.33m
Width: 3.25m
Height: 2.76m
Ground clearance: 0.45m
Maximum road speed: 63km/hour
Maximum road range: 500km

Gradient: 58%
Vertical obstacle: 0.7m
Trench: 2.5m
Armour: 13mm

ARMAMENT:
1x 152mm 2A37 gun (30 rounds)
1x 7.62mm PKT MG

2S7 PION

In the late 1960s, a requirement for a large calibre self-propelled gun was issued. The calibre was not specified, and after studies of various calibres, 203mm was chosen and the 2S7 entered service in 1975. The hull was welded steel, with the driver seated at the front left, and the engine in the front right. When travelling, the commander and gunner were seated in the driver's compartment. The remaining four vehicle crew members were seated to the rear of the engine (another seven crew were carried in the ammunition vehicle). An entrenching blade was fitted to the front of the hull, and an SA-14 surface-to-air missile system was carried.

The 203mm gun was mounted on top of the hull at the rear of the vehicle, with a manually operated travel lock fitted on the hull. A large spade was mounted at the rear, which was used to stabilise the vehicle before firing. Gun traverse and elevation was powered, though manual controls were provided for emergency use. Indirect and direct fire sights were provided for the gunner, who sat to the left of the gun when in action.

The standard HE-FRAG ammunition had a maximum range of 37.5km. Rocket-assisted ammunition was available, which increased maximum range to 47.5km. Concrete-piercing, nuclear, and chemical ammunition was also available. Four rounds

2S7 Pion

were carried on the vehicle, with more ammunition normally carried on a lorry. An ammunition-handling system allowed a rate of fire of two rounds per minute. The vehicle had night-vision equipment and provided the crew with NBC protection when they were inside.

The 2S7M entered service in 1983. This variant carried eight rounds of ammunition on board, had improved durability, and new communications facilities that allowed firing data to be transmitted directly to the gun from the battery commander.

SPECIFICATIONS: 2S7 PION

Crew: 7
Combat weight: 46.5 tonnes
Length: 13.12m including gun
Width: 3.38m
Height: 3m
Ground clearance: 0.4m

Maximum road speed: 50km/hour
Maximum road range: 650km
Gradient: 40%
Vertical obstacle: 0.7m
Trench: 2.5m
Armament: 1x 203mm 2A44 gun (4 rounds, 2S7M: 8 rounds)
Armour: 10mm

2S9 Nona

The 2S9 entered service in 1981, mounting an 120mm gun/mortar in an armoured turret on a BTR-D armoured personnel carrier. Like the BTR-D, it was amphibious, air-droppable, and had NBC protection. It could be used in the indirect and direct fire roles, with HEAT warheads available to provide an anti-tank capability.

The driver sat in the front centre of the hull, with the commander in the front left. The gunner and loader sat in the turret, the gunner on the left, the loader on the right. The turret had limited traverse of 35° either side of directly ahead.

Main armament was a 2A51 120mm gun/mortar, with a rate of fire of six to eight rounds per minute. It could fire HE, HE-RAP, white phosphorous, smoke, and HEAT rounds. Maximum indirect fire range was 8.8km with standard rounds, increased to 13km with rocket-assisted projectiles.

Specifications: 2S9 Nona

Crew: 4
Combat weight: 8.7 tonnes
Length: 6.02m
Width: 2.63m
Height: 1.9m

2S9 Nona

Ground clearance: 0.1m - 0.45m
Maximum road speed: 60km/hour
Maximum road range: 500km
Gradient: 60%
Vertical obstacle: 0.5-0.8m
Trench: 2m
Armament: 1x 120mm 2A60 gun/mortar (25 rounds)
Armour: 16mm

2S19 Msta

The 2S19 entered production and was accepted for service in 1989, as a replacement for both the 2S3 and 2S5. The suspension and running gear were based on those of the T-80 MBT, while the engine was the same as that fitted to the T-72 MBT. The driver's compartment was at the front, the turret extended over the centre and rear of the hull, and the engine was at the rear. The turret and hull were welded steel, and a self-entrenching blade was fitted at the front of the hull.

Main armament was a 2A64 152mm howitzer, which had a fume extractor, double-baffle muzzle brake, and travelling lock. Indirect and direct fire sights were fitted. The gun could fire HE-FRAG and smoke projectiles to a range of 24.7km. Turret traverse and gun elevation were powered, with manual controls for use in an emergency. 50 rounds were carried in the vehicle, though ammunition was normally supplied from outside the vehicle.

A 12.7mm NSVT machine gun and small searchlight were fitted to the roof of the turret, in front of the commander's hatch. Both could be operated remotely from within the vehicle. The 2S19 had NBC protection and passive night-vision equipment. Six smoke grenade dischargers were mounted on the turret, three on each side. A smokescreen could also be generated by injecting diesel fuel into the exhaust.

Specifications: 2S19 Msta

Crew: 5
Combat weight: 42 tonnes
Length: 7.15m (11.92m including gun)
Width: 3.38m
Height: 2.99m
Ground clearance: 0.44m
Maximum road speed: 60km/hour
Maximum road range: 500km
Gradient: 47%
Vertical obstacle: 0.5m
Trench: 2.8m
Armour: Proof against small arms and shell splinters

Tanks and Combat Vehicles of the Warsaw Pact | 167

2S19 Msta

ARMAMENT:
1x 152mm 2A64 howitzer (50 rounds)
1x 12.7mm NSVT MG (300 rounds)

VZOR 77 DANA (CZECHOSLOVAKIA)

This wheeled 152mm self-propelled gun-howitzer was developed in the late 1970s, and entered service with the Czech army in 1981. It had an eight-wheeled chassis based on components of the Tatra 813 8x8 lorry, rather than the more usual tracked chassis. The Tatra 813 had been shown to have a good cross-country capability, but wheeled chassis were much cheaper and easier to maintain than comparable tracked systems. Since the Dana operated some distance behind the lines, tactical mobility was less important than on front-line vehicles.

The driver sat in the front compartment on the left, with the commander to his right. A large, fully enclosed turret was in the centre, with the engine at the rear. Armour was sufficient to provide protection against small arms and shell splinters. A central tyre pressure regulation system and power steering were both fitted.

The driver and commander had roof hatches and windscreens with armoured shutters. Each also had two firing ports, one to the front and one to the side. The commander operated the communication system and was provided with a night sight. The driver operated the turret locking system and stabilisers.

The 152mm gun-howitzer was fitted with a muzzle brake, and could fire the same ammunition as the Soviet 2S3 Akatsiya, as well as Czech-made ammunition. The vehicle had a fully automatic loading system, which loaded the projectile and the separate charge, and could operate at all elevations. Single shot or fully automatic fire modes could be selected by the gunner.

The Dana took two minutes to prepare for firing after coming to a halt, and required one minute to prepare to move off after the last round had been fired. Hydraulic jacks were lowered before firing to ensure a stable platform. Sights were provided for direct fire as well as indirect fire. Up to 60 rounds of ammunition could be carried, but road speed was reduced if more than 40 rounds were carried.

The turret was made up of two distinct parts, with the weapon mounted externally between them, ensuring that no fumes could enter the interior. The turret could only rotate through 225°. Each side of the turret had access doors, roof hatches, and vision devices. The gunner and loader operator were in the left half of the turret, with the ammunition handler, who set the fuses, in the right half.

A 12.7mm anti-aircraft machine gun was fitted to the turret roof on the right side, and could also be used in the direct fire role. An NBC system was fitted as standard.

Specifications: vzor 77 Dana

Crew: 5
Combat weight: 29.25 tonnes
Length: 11.16m
Width: 3m
Height: 2.85m
Ground clearance: 0.41m
Maximum road speed: 80km/hour
Maximum road range: 740km
Gradient: 60%
Vertical obstacle: 0.6m
Trench: 2m

Armament:
1x 152mm gun-howitzer (40 rounds, or 60 rounds with speed reduced to 70km/hour)
1x 12.7mm NSV MG

Multiple Rocket Launchers

The Soviet Union pioneered the use of the self-propelled multiple rocket launcher (MRL) during the Second World War, when they were officially known as Guards Mortars, but commonly known by the nickname Katyusha. The ease of construction compared to tube artillery (which requires complex tools for rifling barrels) meant that mass production was possible even after the Germans overran many of the armaments factories.

The simple expedient of mounting the rockets on lorries or other vehicles allowed them to move immediately after firing to avoid counter-battery fire, a significant problem given the large launch signature and long reloading time. The ability to deliver a large quantity of explosive in a short time made them ideal for laying down suppressive fire to minimise the effectiveness of enemy ATGMs and artillery.

BM-24

The BM-24 entered service in 1951. It had a crew of six and mounted twelve 240mm rockets on an elevating launcher with limited traverse. Elevation and traverse was manual, and two stabilising jacks had to be lowered before launch. The launch frames were arranged in two rows of six, mounted on the rear of a ZIL-151 6x6 chassis. Steel plates were fitted above the cab and

BM-24

fuel tanks to protect them from the blast when the rockets were fired. The system could fire two types of HE rocket: the M-24F with 27.4kg of explosive, and the M-24FUD, which had a lighter payload of 18.4kg but extended the range from 6km to 10.6km. It could also fire MS-24 and MS-24D rockets, fitted with chemical warheads.

In 1956, a new rocket, the MD-24F, was introduced. This had a maximum range of 17.5km.

The BM-24T variant entered service in 1956. It used the AT-S artillery tractor as the base for the launch vehicle, and was issued to tank divisions, with the wheeled BM-24 going to motor rifle divisions. The BM-24 had open frame launchers, the BM-24T enclosed tubes.

Specifications: BM-24 Vehicle

Weight: 9.2 tonnes
Length: 6.71m
Width: 2.32m
Height: 2.91m
Maximum road speed: 65km/hour
Range: 430km
Number of launchers: 12
Reload time: 3-4 minutes
Traverse: 140°
Elevation: 0 to +65°

Specifications: BM-24T Vehicle

Weight: 15.24 tonnes
Length: 5.87m
Width: 2.57m
Height: 3.1m
Maximum road speed: 35km/hour
Range: 380km
Number of launchers: 12
Reload time: 3-4 minutes
Traverse: 210°
Elevation: 0 to +45°

Specifications: BM-24 Rocket

Rocket calibre: 240mm
Warhead weight: 46.9kg
Rocket length: 1.18m
Rocket weight: 112.5kg
Rocket range: up to 17.5km, depending on rocket type

BMD-20

Development of a 200mm rocket for what was to become the BMD-20 started in 1945. Several changes to the requirements led to delays. Trials were carried out in 1951, and the BMD-20 entered service in 1952, mounting four 200mm rockets in a single row on the back of a ZIL-151 6x6 chassis. Two jacks were lowered before firing to improve stability of the launch platform. The rockets were housed in open framework tubes on a manually operated mounting with limited traverse. The rockets had 30kg HE-FRAG warheads and a maximum range of 19km.

SPECIFICATIONS: BMD-20

Weight: 8.7 tonnes
Length: 7.2m
Width: 2.3m
Height: 2.85m
Maximum road speed: 60km/hour
Range: 600km
Rocket calibre: 200mm
Number of launchers: 4
Warhead weight: 30kg
Rocket length: 3.11m
Rocket weight: 91.4kg
Rocket range: 19km
Reload time: 10 minutes
Traverse: 200°
Elevation: 0 to +50°

BM-14

The BM-14 (also known as BM-14-16) entered service in 1952 as a replacement for the wartime BM-13. It had sixteen

BM-14

140mm rockets, in two rows of eight, on a mounting with limited traverse. Elevation and traverse was manual, and the mounting was fitted on a ZIS-151 6x6 chassis. A remote firing mechanism was provided, allowing the operator to fire the rockets from up to 60m away from the vehicle. Initially only HE-FRAG warheads were available, but smoke (WP) and chemical warheads were introduced in 1955. Later models used ZIL-157 (BM-14M) and ZIL-131 (BM-14MM) chassis in place of the original ZIS-151.

In 1959, the BM-14-17 was introduced, which had 17 launch tubes on a GAZ-63A 4x4 chassis. A towed variant, the RPU-14, was produced for use with the airborne forces. This had 16 tubes in four rows of four, mounted on a carriage similar to that used by the D-44 85mm gun. It was replaced by the BM-21V.

SPECIFICATIONS: BM-14-16 VEHICLE

Weight: 8.2 tonnes
Length: 9.92m
Width: 2.3m
Height: 2.65m
Maximum road speed: 60km/hour
Range: 600km
Number of launchers: 16

Traverse: 200°
Elevation: 0 to +52°

Specifications: BM-14-17 Vehicle

Weight: 5.3 tonnes
Length: 5.41m
Width: 1.93m
Height: 2.24m
Maximum road speed: 65km/hour
Range: 650km
Number of launchers: 17
Traverse: 210°
Elevation: 0 to +47°

Specifications: BM-14 Rocket

Rocket calibre: 140mm
Warhead weight: 18.8kg
Rocket length: 1.08m
Rocket weight: 39.6kg
Rocket range: 9.8km
Reload time: 4 minutes

BM-25

The BM-25 entered service in 1957, and had six liquid-fuelled 255mm rockets in open-frame launchers. The launchers were mounted in two rows of three on a KrAZ-214 6x6 chassis. Before firing, two stabilisers were lowered and armoured shutters were fitted over the windscreens. A tarpaulin normally covered the launch assembly while in transit.

Specifications: BM-25

Weight: 18.15 tonnes
Length: 9.82m
Width: 2.7m
Height: 3.5m
Maximum road speed: 55km/hour
Range: 530km
Rocket calibre: 250mm
Number of launchers: 6
Rocket length: 5.82m
Rocket weight: 455kg
Rocket range: 30km
Reload time: 10-20 minutes
Traverse: 6°
Elevation: 0 to +55°

BM-21 Grad

Developed during the mid-to-late 1950s, the BM-21 entered service in 1963, with the designation BM-21 (known in the West as BM-21a). Each division was equipped with a battalion of 12 launchers, and each army or front had three battalions. In wartime, all battalions were to be increased in size to 18 launchers.

The launch vehicle was based on a Ural-375D 6x6 chassis, fitted with an elevating, rotating assembly on the rear bed, carrying 40 launch tubes in four rows of ten. The launch assembly was rotated forward for travelling. Stabilisers were fitted to each side of the vehicle at the rear and were lowered to the ground before firing. The cabin contained all the equipment needed to prepare and fire the rockets, which could be fired individually, in a salvo, or by selective ripple. A remote-control

BM-21 Grad

unit was provided, allowing the crew to fire the rockets from a distance of up to 60m from the vehicle. Initially only HE-FRAG warheads were available, but incendiary and chemical warheads were subsequently developed.

Later, the Ural-4320 6x6 chassis was used as the base vehicle, and this variant was given the designation BM-21-1. This version also had an automated fire control system and a satellite navigation system.

In 1969, the BM-21V was developed for use by airborne forces. This was much lighter, mounting a 12-tube launcher on a GAZ-66B 4x4 chassis. Like the BM-21, two stabilisers had to be lowered before firing, and rockets could be fired individually or in a salvo. In order to facilitate air transport and dropping by parachute, the cab was collapsible, the steering wheel was telescopic, and the doors and windscreen could be removed. There were tie-down points for attaching the vehicle to a pallet for dropping by parachute.

The BM-21b Grad-1 entered service in 1976 as a lightweight, regimental-level system for use in independent MRL batteries. The basic arrangement was the same as the original BM-21, but with 36 launch tubes (the lower two rows had eight tubes each instead of 10) mounted on the rear of a ZIL-131 chassis. This variant fired a different rocket with shorter range but more effective warhead (the HE-FRAG warhead was preformed, and the incendiary warhead carried more incendiary elements).

Specifications: BM-21 Grad

Weight: 13.7 tonnes
Length: 7.35m
Width: 2.69m
Height: 2.85m
Maximum road speed: 75km/hour
Range: 480km
Rocket calibre: 122mm
Number of launchers: 40
Warhead weight: 19.4kg
Rocket length: 3.22m
Rocket weight: 77.5kg
Rocket range: 20.5km
Reload time: 10 minutes
Traverse: 180°
Elevation: 0 to +55°

Specifications: BM-21b Grad-1

Weight: 10.5 tonnes
Length: 6.9m
Width: 2.5m
Height: 2.48m

Maximum road speed: 80km/hour

Range: 525km

Rocket calibre: 122mm

Number of launchers: 36

Warhead weight: 18.4kg

Rocket length: 2.87m

Rocket weight: 66kg

Rocket range: 20km

Reload time: 10 minutes

Traverse: 180°

Elevation: 0 to +55°

BM-27 Uragan

Development of the BM-27 was completed in 1975, and it was accepted for service in the same year. It was sometimes mistakenly referred to as the BM-22 in the West. It was deployed in regiments (three battalions) or brigades (four battalions) at army or front level. Each battalion had 12 launch vehicles, but in wartime would receive an extra six. Each battalion had a Kapustnik-B automated fire control system, comprising a commander's vehicle based on the BTR-80 chassis, a chief of staff vehicle based on a Ural-4320 chassis, three battery command vehicles based on BTR-80 chassis, and three battery senior officer vehicles based on the Ural-4320 chassis. The Kapustnik-B included systems for reconnaissance, initial battalion orientation, location fixing, weather reconnaissance, ballistic tracking, communications, and data transfer.

The BM-27 launch vehicle was based on the same ZIL-135LM 8x8 chassis as the FROG-7 tactical ballistic missile. The crew compartment was not armoured, but did provide NBC protection. 16 tubes were arranged in three rows on an elevating mount at

BM-27 Uragan

the rear with limited traverse. The top row had four tubes, while the lower two rows had six tubes each. Launch preparation and firing equipment were in the cab, where the operator could choose between firing a full salvo or individual rockets. Before firing, two stabilisers were lowered and a steel shutter was fitted over the windscreen.

The 9T452 transloader vehicle was based on the same chassis as the launch vehicle. Each one carried 16 rockets in two stacks, either side of a hydraulic crane fitted in the centre of the rear deck. For loading, the launcher was traversed to one side and put into the horizontal position.

Specifications: BM-27 Uragan

Weight: 20 tonnes
Length: 9.63m
Width: 2.8m
Height: 3.23m
Maximum road speed: 65km/hour
Range: 570km

Rocket calibre: 220mm
Number of launchers: 16
Warhead weight: 51.7kg
Rocket length: 4.83m
Rocket weight: 280kg
Rocket range: 35km
Reload time: 20-30 minutes
Traverse: 60°
Elevation: 0 to +55°

BM-30 Smerch

Development of the BM-30 started during the late 1970s, and the system entered service in 1987. The launch vehicle was based on the MAZ-543A 8x8 chassis, with a 12-round elevating, rotating launcher. The launch tubes were arranged as a row of four on top, with a pair of 2x2 blocks underneath, one on each side of the elevating assembly. Two stabilisers were fitted, which had to be lowered before firing. The cabin contained the launch preparation and firing equipment. The rockets could be fired individually or as a salvo. Each launch vehicle had an associated 9T234-2 transloader vehicle, based on the same MAZ-543A chassis, with 12 reload rockets and a hydraulic crane to facilitate loading.

BM-30s were organised into batteries of four launchers, with three batteries to a battalion. Each battery had a command vehicle and a staff vehicle, both based on the KamAZ-4310 6x6 chassis. These vehicles contained communications equipment, digital computers, and the Vivariy automated fire control system.

The rockets had a flight-control system to allow them to correct their trajectory in flight, leading to greatly improved

BM-30 Smerch

accuracy, claimed to be 0.21% of range. High explosive and cluster munition warheads were available.

SPECIFICATIONS: BM-30 SMERCH

Weight: 43.7 tonnes
Length: 12.1m
Width: 3.05m
Height: 3.05m
Maximum road speed: 60km/hour
Range: 850km
Rocket calibre: 300mm
Number of launchers: 12
Warhead weight: 92.5kg
Rocket length: 7.6m
Rocket weight: 800kg
Rocket range: 70km
Reload time: 36 minutes

Traverse: 60°
Elevation: 0 to +55°

BM 9A51 Prima

The BM 9A51 was developed in the early to mid-1980s, and entered service in 1987. It was primarily assigned to divisions, in battalions of 12 vehicles, which would be expanded to 18 vehicles in wartime, but was sometimes found at army or front level in place of the BM-21.

The BM 9A51 used the same Ural-4320 6x6 chassis as the BM-21-1, but mounted 50 launch tubes in a rotating, elevating mount on the rear. The tubes were arranged in five rows of 10, within a box structure. Two stabilisers were fitted on the sides, toward the rear, which had to be lowered before firing. Aiming and launching could be controlled from within the cab, or from outside the vehicle, using a remote-control unit. 72 reloads were carried on a 9T232M transloader vehicle, also based on the Ural-4320 chassis. Reloading took around 10 minutes.

The BM 9A51 could fire the same 122mm rockets as the BM-21, but a new rocket, the 9M53F, was developed specifically for it. This rocket had a HE-FRAG warhead that separated and descended below a small parachute, then detonated several yards above the ground. The combination of air burst and near-vertical descent due to the use of a parachute resulted in a wider blast radius than the more usual ground burst. If required, the fuse could be set to enable conventional operation, with the warhead remaining with the rocket and detonating on contact with the ground.

Specifications: BM 9A51 Prima

Weight: 13.9 tonnes
Length: 7.35m
Width: 2.43m
Height: 2.68m
Maximum road speed: 85km/hour
Range: 990km
Rocket calibre: 122mm
Number of launchers: 50
Warhead weight: 26kg
Rocket length: 3.04m
Rocket weight: 70kg
Rocket range: 20.5km
Reload time: 10 minutes
Traverse: 58°
Elevation: 0 to +55°

RM-51 (Czechoslovakia)

The RM-51, sometimes referred to as the RM-130, entered service with the Czech army in 1956. It mounted 32 rockets on the back of a Praga V3S 6x6 lorry in four rows of eight. The 130mm rockets were spin stabilised, and the launcher had to be traversed to one side before firing, since the unarmoured cab had no protection from back blast. Stowage boxes for spare rockets were fitted on either side of the hull, under the launcher.

The standard version was used by Czechoslovakia and exported to Bulgaria, Cuba, and Egypt. The Austrian army used the RM-51 launcher mounted on Steyr 680 M3 6x6 lorries, and the Romanian army used it mounted on Soviet ZIL-151 or ZIL-157 lorries.

RM-51

SPECIFICATIONS: RM-51

Weight: 8.9 tonnes
Length: 6.91m
Width: 2.31m
Height: 2.92m
Maximum road speed: 62km/hour
Range: 440km
Rocket calibre: 130mm
Number of launchers: 32
Warhead weight: 2.3kg
Rocket length: 0.8m
Rocket weight: 24.2kg
Rocket range: 8.2km
Reload time: 2 minutes
Traverse: 240°
Elevation: 0 to +50°

RM-70 (CZECHOSLOVAKIA)

First observed by the West at a 1972 parade, the RM-70 was based on a Czech Tatra 813 8x8 lorry. It had the same launcher as the Soviet BM-21 at the rear of the vehicle, but unlike the Soviet vehicle, an extra set of 40 rockets was carried between the launcher and the cab, to allow for rapid reloading. The cab was fully armoured, providing the crew with protection from small arms fire and shell splinters, and the Tatra chassis provided much better cross-country capability than the Ural-375D 6x6 chassis used by the BM-21. A central tyre pressure regulation system was fitted, allowing the driver to adjust the tyre pressure according to the ground being crossed.

An improved version, the Mod 70/85, was introduced in the mid-1980s. This used the more modern Tatra T815 VNN 8x8 chassis, with the same launcher and reloads. The cab was not armoured, but it did have a central tyre pressure regulation system and NBC protection for the crew of four.

SPECIFICATIONS: RM-70 (RM-70/85 IN BRACKETS)

Weight: 25.3 tonnes (25 tonnes)
Length: 8.8m (9.6m)
Width: 2.55m (2.53m)
Height: 2.96m (3.03m)
Maximum road speed: 75km/hour (60km/hour)
Range: 1,100km (1,000km)
Rocket calibre: 122mm
Number of launchers: 40
Warhead weight: 19.4kg
Rocket length: 3.22m
Rocket weight: 77.5kg
Rocket range: 20.5km

Reload time: 35 seconds
Traverse: 125° left, 70° right
Elevation: 0 to +55°

Tactical Ballistic Missiles

When Khrushchev came to power following Stalin's death, he ordered major cuts in conventional forces, as he intended to rely on nuclear missiles for defence. The new leader was a great believer in the relatively new technology of missiles, and this led to greater use of missiles throughout the Soviet military, as it was easier to secure funding for missile systems than for gun systems. Under Khrushchev, the Soviet Union sought to build up its nuclear missile forces at all levels, from tactical systems to intercontinental ballistic missiles.

FROG-1

The first two vehicles of the FROG (Free Rocket Over Ground) series, the FROG-1 and FROG-2, entered service in 1955. The FROG-1 carried a rocket with a solid fuel engine and a maximum range of 25.7km. It could be fitted with a tactical nuclear warhead or a 1,200kg HE-FRAG warhead. The launch vehicle was based on a modified IS-2 tank chassis.

Specifications: FROG-1

Vehicle weight: 36 tonnes
Vehicle length: 9.33m
Vehicle width: 3.07m

Vehicle height: 3m
Vehicle road speed: 30km/hour (41km/hour without a rocket)
Vehicle road range: 150km
Missile length: 10.2m
Missile diameter: 612mm
Missile weight: 3,200kg
Missile range: 25.7km
Missile CEP: 700m

FROG-2

The FROG-2 had a non-amphibious chassis based on that of the PT-76 light tank. It carried a solid fuel powered rocket with a maximum range of 17.5km. The rocket was fitted with a conventional high explosive warhead.

FROG-2

Specifications: FROG-2

Vehicle weight: 16.4 tonnes
Vehicle length: 9.4m
Vehicle width: 3.18m
Vehicle height: 3.05m
Vehicle road speed: 20km/hour (40km/hour without a rocket)
Vehicle road range: 250km
Missile length: 9.01m
Missile diameter: 324mm
Missile weight: 1,760kg
Missile range: 17.5km
Missile CEP: 770m

FROG-3/4/5

The FROG-3, FROG-4 and FROG-5 were given different designations by NATO, but were in fact the same system, with different warheads on the rockets. They entered service with the Soviet army in 1960, under the designation 2K6 Luna. The chassis was based on that of the FROG-2. The vehicles weighed 18.8 tonnes and had a maximum speed of 40km/hour. The rockets could be fitted with HE-FRAG (FROG-3), chemical (FROG-4), or tactical nuclear (FROG-5) warheads.

The launch vehicles were reloaded from ZIL-157 6x6 lorries, each towing a trailer with two reload rockets, and a separate crane lorry to lift the rockets onto the launch vehicles. Each launch vehicle had a crew of 11.

Specifications: FROG-3/4/5

Vehicle weight: 18.8 tonnes
Vehicle length: 10.5m
Vehicle width: 3.1m

FROG-3

Vehicle height: 3.05m
Vehicle road speed: 40 km/hour
Missile length: 10.6m
Missile diameter: 540mm
Missile weight: 2,280kg
Missile range: 45km-61km depending on warhead
Missile CEP: 800m

FROG-7

In 1964, a new missile system was accepted for service, designated FROG-7a by NATO. This was a solid fuel powered rocket mounted on a wheeled TEL vehicle based on the ZIL-135LM 8x8 chassis. A range of different warheads were available. As well as high explosive, chemical, and nuclear warheads, a leaflet-dispensing warhead was produced. An air-mobile version, with the rocket mounted on a self-propelled trailer, did not got

FROG-7

past the prototype stage. The FROG-7b entered service in 1968, with improvements to the rocket and a longer warhead, increasing rocket length from 8.95m to 9.4m. Cluster munition warheads, with 42 HE bomblets, were available for the FROG-7b. There were three types of nuclear warhead for the FROG-7: the AA-22 and AA-38 had selectable yields of 3, 10 or 22kT; and the AA-52 had a selectable yield of 5, 10, 20 or 200kT. The HE warhead carried 450kg of explosive.

Unlike previous vehicles, the FROG-7 TEL had an on-board hydraulic crane for loading rockets. Reloads were carried on a similar vehicle, with three rockets on each. It took around 15-30 minutes to prepare to fire, and around 20 minutes to reload. Maximum flight time was around 160 seconds, with the engine burning for 7-11 seconds.

SPECIFICATIONS: FROG-7 (FROG-7B IN BRACKETS)

Vehicle weight: 19 tonnes
Vehicle length: 10.69m
Vehicle width: 2.8m
Vehicle height: 3.35m

Vehicle road speed: 65 km/hour
Vehicle road range: 650 km
Missile length: 8.95m (9.4m)
Missile diameter: 0.5m
Missile weight: 2,432 - 2,450kg
Missile range: 70km
Missile CEP: 400m

SS-1 Scud

The SS-1b Scud A entered service in 1957. Unlike the FROG series, it employed gyroscopes to provide a rudimentary guidance system. Guidance commands were only issued during powered flight and the missiles were unguided once the rocket ran out of fuel, after around 80 seconds. This resulted in poor accuracy, especially at longer ranges. The SS-1b was carried on a TEL vehicle with a tracked chassis derived from the IS-3 tank. Maximum range was 150km.

The SS-1c Scud B entered service in 1961, initially mounted on the same TEL vehicle as the SS-1b, though in 1965, a new wheeled TEL based on the MAZ-543 was introduced. This model had an improved rocket with a new engine. Maximum range was increased to 300km, and accuracy was improved. Nuclear, chemical, and HE warheads were available. The launch sequence could be controlled from the TEL, but was normally done from a command vehicle. Time to prepare and launch was around one hour.

Specifications: SS-1b Scud A

Vehicle weight: 38 tonnes
Vehicle length: 12.5m
Vehicle width: 3.2m

SS-1c Scud B

Vehicle height: 3.32m
Vehicle road speed: 37km/hour
Missile length: 10.7m
Missile diameter: 0.88m
Missile weight: 4,400kg
Missile range: 180km
Missile CEP: 3km

Specifications: SS-1c Scud B

Vehicle weight: 29 tonnes
Vehicle length: 13.58m
Vehicle width: 3.02m
Vehicle height: 3.7m
Vehicle road speed: 70km/hour
Missile length: 11.25m
Missile diameter: 0.88m
Missile weight: 5,900kg

Missile range: 300km
Missile CEP: 450m

SS-12 Scaleboard

The SS-12 Scaleboard was the longest-ranged ballistic missile to serve with the Soviet ground forces. It entered service in 1969, mounting a single missile inside a container on the same MAZ-543 chassis as the SS-1c Scud B. In 1979, a new missile, the SS-12M Scaleboard B (initially known in the West as the SS-22) began to replace the original missiles. The TEL was the same, but accuracy was improved. Under the terms of the 1987 INF Treaty, these missiles were destroyed between August 1988 and July 1989.

SS-12 Scaleboard

Specifications: SS-12 Scaleboard (SS-12M in brackets)

Vehicle weight: 30.8 tonnes
Vehicle length: 13.15m
Vehicle width: 3.02m
Vehicle height: 3.5m
Vehicle road speed: 70km/hour
Missile length: 12.78m
Missile diameter: 1.01m
Missile weight: 9,800kg
Missile range: 800km (900km)
Missile CEP: 750m (370m)

SS-21 Scarab

The SS-21 Scarab entered service in 1976, as a replacement for the FROG-7. The TEL was a six-wheeled vehicle with amphibious capability and NBC protection for the crew, with the missile contained in a temperature-controlled unit until launch. The missile was powered by a solid fuel rocket motor, and was guided throughout the entire flight. The crew could perform all tasks related to targeting and launching the missile from within the cab. High explosive, chemical, and nuclear warheads were available, with the AA-60 nuclear warhead having a selectable yield of 5, 10, 20 or 200kT. In 1989, the Scarab B was introduced, with a longer range and better accuracy. A separate transloader vehicle carried two additional missiles, and had a crane for loading missiles onto the launch vehicle.

Specifications: SS-21 Scarab (Scarab B in brackets)

Vehicle weight: 18.15 tonnes
Vehicle length: 9.48m

SS-21 Scarab

Vehicle width: 2.78m
Vehicle height: 2.35m
Vehicle road speed: 60 km/hour
Vehicle road range: 650km
Missile length: 6.4m
Missile diameter: 0.65m
Missile weight: 2,000kg (2,010kg)
Missile range: 70km (120km)
Missile CEP: 160m (95m)

SS-23 Spider

The SS-23 Spider entered service in 1980, replacing the SS-1c Scud B. The TEL vehicle was based on the 8x8 BAZ-6944 chassis. It had NBC protection for the crew and was fully amphibious, propelled in the water by a pair of water jets. When in transit, the missile was contained within the vehicle. The crew did not need to leave the cab to prepare and launch the missile, which took around 5-10 minutes.

The missile had a single solid fuel rocket motor, with inertial and active radar terminal guidance, providing a high level of accuracy. It missile was difficult to intercept, and the high level of

SS-23 Spider

accuracy meant that use against moving or hardened targets was feasible. A transporter-loader was based on the same chassis, and carried a single reload missile with a loading crane. High explosive (450kg), chemical, submunition, and nuclear (AA-60, as used on SS-21) warheads were available.

When the INF Treaty was signed in 1987, the United States claimed that the SS-23 was covered by the treaty, since they had estimated the range to be at least 500km. The Soviet Union maintained that maximum range was less than 500km and that the system was therefore not covered. None the less, as a gesture of goodwill, all existing systems were destroyed and work on an improved version was cancelled.

SPECIFICATIONS: SS-23 SPIDER

Vehicle weight: 24.7 tonnes
Vehicle length: 11.76m
Vehicle width: 3.13m

Vehicle height: 3m
Vehicle road speed: 70 km/hour
Vehicle road range: 700km
Missile length: 7.5m
Missile diameter: 0.9m
Missile weight: 4,500 - 5,000kg
Missile range: 50-480km
Missile CEP: 30-150m

Glossary

AA: Anti-Aircraft
AP: Armour Piercing
APC: Armoured Personnel Carrier. An armoured vehicle used to transport infantry, usually lightly armed and armoured
APDS: Armour Piercing Discarding Sabot. A type of kinetic energy anti-tank round fired from rifled guns
APFSDS: Armour Piercing Fin Stabilised Discarding Sabot. A type of kinetic energy anti-tank round, usually fired from smoothbore guns
ATGM: Anti-Tank Guided Missile
ATGW: Anti-Tank Guided Weapon
BMD: Boevaya Mashina Desantnaya (Airborne Combat Vehicle)
BMP: Boevaya Mashina Pekhota (Infantry Combat Vehicle)
BRM: Boevaya Razvedyvatnaya Mashina (Combat Reconnaissance Vehicle)
CEP: Circular Error of Probability. A measure of accuracy, the CEP was the radius of a circle within which 50% of projectiles would fall
ECCM: Electronic Counter-Counter Measures
ECM: Electronic Counter Measures
ERA: Explosive Reactive Armour
GSFG: Group of Soviet Forces Germany. The Soviet forces based in East Germany
HE: High Explosive

HE-RAP: High Explosive Rocket Assisted Projectile. A HE projectile with a small rocket motor to boost range

HEAT: High Explosive Anti-Tank. A form of chemical energy anti-tank warhead commonly used on anti-tank missiles

HEAT-FS: High Explosive Anti-Tank - Fin Stabilised

HE-FRAG: High Explosive Fragmentation

HESH: High Explosive Squash Head. A form of chemical energy anti-tank warhead, particularly favoured by the British army

IFF: Identification Friend or Foe. A system to automatically identify friendly aircraft

IFV: Infantry Fighting Vehicle. Similar to an APC, but with greater armament, intended to provide support to the dismounted infantry

MBT: Main Battle Tank

MCLOS: Manual Command Line-Of-Sight. First generation anti-tank missile guidance system, which required the operator to manually steer the missile to the target

MRL: Multiple Rocket Launcher

Muzzle brake: A device fitted to the muzzle of a gun to redirect propellant gasses, reducing recoil

NBC: Nuclear, Biological, and Chemical

SACLOS: Semi-Automatic Command Line-Of-Sight. Second generation anti-tank missile guidance system, which simply required the operator to keep the target in the system's sight

SAM: Surface-to-Air Missile

SPG: Self-Propelled Gun

TEL: Transporter, Erector, Launcher. A vehicle on which one or more missiles were transported, and from which the missiles were launched

TELAR: Transporter, Erector, Launcher, and Radar. A TEL vehicle with integrated radar

WP: White Phosphorous

Image Credits

Tanks

T-34/85: Vitaly V. Kuzmin (CC-BY-SA 4.0 International)
T-10M: Alex-engraver (CC-BY-SA 3.0 Unported)
T-54: Vitaly V. Kuzmin (CC-BY-SA 4.0 International)
T-55: John Kearney
T-62: John Kearney
T-64BV: Andrew Bossi (CC-BY-SA 2.5 Generic)
T-72A: Vitaly V. Kuzmin (CC-BY-SA 4.0 International)
T-80U: Vitaly V. Kuzmin (CC-BY-SA 4.0 International)
TR-85: Brigada 15 Mecanizată (www.bg15mc.ro) (CC-BY-SA 3.0 Unported)

Infantry Fighting Vehicles

BMP-1: Vitaly V. Kuzmin (CC-BY-SA 4.0 International)
BMP-2: Vitaly V. Kuzmin (CC-BY-SA 4.0 International)
BMP-3: Vitaly V. Kuzmin (CC-BY-SA 4.0 International)
BMD-1: Vitaly V. Kuzmin (CC-BY-SA 4.0 International)
BMD-2: Vitaly V. Kuzmin (CC-BY-SA 4.0 International)
Dismounting from an MLI-84: MAPN (CC-BY-SA 3.0 Unported)

Armoured Personnel Carriers

BTR-40: Bukvoed (CC-BY-SA 3.0 Unported)
BTR-50P: ShinePhantom (CC-BY-SA 3.0 Unported)
BTR-70: Vitaly V. Kuzmin (CC-BY-SA 4.0 International)
BTR-D prepared for parachute drop: Vitaly V. Kuzmin (CC-BY-SA 4.0 International)
MT-LB: Vitaly V. Kuzmin (CC-BY-SA 4.0 International)
TAB-77: Locotenent-Colonel Dragoş Anghelache (CC-BY-SA 3.0 Unported)

Anti-Tank Vehicles

SU-100: Vitaly V. Kuzmin (CC-BY-SA 4.0 International)
ASU-57 with Ch-51 gun: Vitaly V. Kuzmin (CC-BY-SA 4.0 International)
ASU-85: Vitaly V. Kuzmin (CC-BY-SA 4.0 International)
2P26: High Contrast (CC-BY-SA 3.0 Germany)
2P27: Vitaly V. Kuzmin (CC-BY-SA 4.0 International)
IT-1: Vitaly V. Kuzmin (CC-BY-SA 4.0 International)
9P149: Vitaly V. Kuzmin (CC-BY-SA 4.0 International)

Reconnaissance Vehicles

BRDM-1 with extra wheels lowered: Vitaly V. Kuzmin (CC-BY-SA 4.0 International)
BRM: Vitaly V. Kuzmin (CC-BY-SA 4.0 International)

Self-Propelled Anti-Aircraft Weapons

ZSU-57-2: VargaA (CC-BY-SA 4.0 International)
ZSU-23-4 Shilka: Vitaly V. Kuzmin (CC-BY-SA 4.0 International)
2S6M: Vitaly V. Kuzmin (CC-BY-SA 4.0 International)
SA-4 Ganef: ShinePhantom (CC-BY-SA 3.0 Unported)

SA-6 Gainful: Vitaly V. Kuzmin (CC-BY-SA 4.0 International)
SA-8 Gecko: Sevda Babayeva (CC-BY-SA 3.0 Unported)
SA-12 Gladiator: Vitaly V. Kuzmin (CC-BY-SA 4.0 International)
SA-13 Gopher: Srđan Popović (CC-BY-SA 4.0 International)
BTR-ZD: Serge Serebro, Vitebsk Popular News (CC-BY-SA 3.0 Unported)
M53/59: Kaufi (CC-BY-SA 3.0 Unported)

Self-Propelled Guns, Howitzers, and Mortars

ISU-122: Taw (CC-BY-SA 3.0 Unported)
ISU-152: Vitaly V. Kuzmin (CC-BY-SA 4.0 International)
2S1 Gvozdika: Vitaly V. Kuzmin (CC-BY-SA 4.0 International)
2S3 Akatsiya: Vitaly V. Kuzmin (CC-BY-SA 4.0 International)
2S4 Tyulpan: Vitaly V. Kuzmin (CC-BY-SA 4.0 International)
2S5 Giatsint-S in firing position: Parutip (CC-BY-SA 3.0 Unported)
2S7 Pion: Vitaly V. Kuzmin (CC-BY-SA 4.0 International)

Multiple Rocket Launchers

BM-24: Bukvoed (CC-BY-SA 3.0 Unported)
BM-14: (CC-BY 3.0 Unported)
BM-30 Smerch: Vitaly V. Kuzmin (CC-BY-SA 4.0 International)
RM-51: Tourbillon (CC-BY 3.0 Unported)

Tactical Ballistic Missiles

FROG-3: Leonidl (CC-BY-SA 3.0 Unported)
FROG-7: Vitaly V. Kuzmin (CC-BY-SA 4.0 International)
SS-12 Scaleboard: Vitaly V. Kuzmin (CC-BY-SA 4.0 International)
SS-21 Scarab: Gulustan (CC-BY-SA 3.0 Unported)

Digital Reinforcements: Free Ebook

To get a free ebook of this title, simply scan the code below, or go to www.shilka.co.uk/dr and enter code WPTC12.

The free ebook can be downloaded in several formats: Mobi (for Kindle devices & apps), ePub (for other ereaders & ereader apps), and PDF (for reading on a computer). Ereader apps are available for all computers, tablets and smartphones.

About Russell Phillips

Russell Phillips writes books and articles about military technology and history. His articles have been published in Miniature Wargames, Wargames Illustrated, and the Society of Twentieth Century Wargamers' Journal. Some of these articles are available on his website. He has been interviewed on BBC Radio Stoke and The Voice of Russia.

To get advance notice of new books, join Russell's mailing list at www.rpbook.co.uk/list. You can unsubscribe at any time.

For a full listing of Russell's books, go to www.rpbook.co.uk/books.

Find Russell Phillips Online

Website: www.rpbook.co.uk
Twitter: @RPBook
Facebook: RussellPhillipsBooks
Goodreads: RussellPhillips
E-mail: russell@rpbook.co.uk
Join Russell's mailing list: www.rpbook.co.uk/list

Index

Introduction ... 1
Tanks ... 5
    T-34/85 ... 6
    T-44 ... 8
    IS-3 ... 10
    IS-10/T-10 ... 13
    PT-76 ... 15
    T-54 ... 17
    T-55 ... 20
    T-62 ... 23
    T-64 ... 26
    T-72 ... 29
    T-80 ... 33
    TR-77-580 (Romania) ... 36
    TR-85 (Romania) ... 37
Infantry Fighting Vehicles ... 39
    BMP-1 ... 39
    BMP-2 ... 42
    BMP-3 ... 45
    BMD-1 ... 46
    BMD-2 ... 49
    BMD-3 ... 50
    BMP-23 (Bulgaria) ... 52
    MLI-84 (Romania) ... 54
Armoured Personnel Carriers ... 57
    BTR-40 ... 57
    BTR-152 ... 59
    BTR-50P ... 61
    BTR-60P ... 63

    BTR-70 66
    BTR-80 68
    BTR-D 70
    MT-LB 72
    OT-810 (Czechoslovakia) 74
    OT-62 (Czechoslovakia/Poland) 76
    OT-64/SKOT (Czechoslovakia/Poland) 79
    PSZH-IV (Hungary) 82
    TAB-71 (Romania) 84
    TAB-77 (Romania) 85
    MLVM Mountaineers Combat Vehicle (Romania) 87
Anti-Tank Vehicles 89
    SU-100 90
    SU-122-54 92
    ASU-57 93
    ASU-85 94
    2P26 96
    2P27 97
    2P32 99
    9P110 100
    IT-1 102
    9P124 104
    9P122 105
    9P148 107
    9P149 109
Reconnaissance Vehicles 111
    BRDM-1 111
    BRDM-2 113
    BRM 115
    BRM-23 (Bulgaria) 117
    FÚG (Hungary) 118
Self-Propelled Anti-Aircraft Weapons 121

BTR-40A & BTR-152A..121
ZSU-57-2...123
ZSU-23-4 Shilka..124
2S6..126
SA-4 Ganef..128
SA-6 Gainful..130
SA-8 Gecko..132
SA-9 Gaskin...134
SA-10 Grumble..136
SA-11 Gadfly..137
SA-12 Gladiator...139
SA-13 Gopher...140
BTR-ZD...142
M53/59 (Czechoslovakia)..144

Self-Propelled Guns, Howitzers, and Mortars.....................147
SU-76..147
ISU-122..150
ISU-152..152
2S1 Gvozdika..153
2S3 Akatsiya..155
2S4 Tyulpan...158
2S5 Giatsint-S..160
2S7 Pion...162
2S9 Nona..164
2S19 Msta..165
vzor 77 Dana (Czechoslovakia)..................................167

Multiple Rocket Launchers...171
BM-24...171
BMD-20...174
BM-14...174
BM-25...176
BM-21 Grad..177

BM-27 Uragan..180
BM-30 Smerch..182
BM 9A51 Prima..184
RM-51 (Czechoslovakia)...185
RM-70 (Czechoslovakia)..187
Tactical Ballistic Missiles...189
FROG-1..189
FROG-2..190
FROG-3/4/5...191
FROG-7..192
SS-1 Scud...194
SS-12 Scaleboard...196
SS-21 Scarab...197
SS-23 Spider...198
Glossary...201
Image Credits..203
Digital Reinforcements: Free Ebook....................................207
About Russell Phillips...209
Find Russell Phillips Online..209

www.ingramcontent.com/pod-product-compliance
Lightning Source LLC
Chambersburg PA
CBHW020612300426
44113CB00007B/617